A GUIDE
TO
HOUSING LAW

Roger Sproston

British Library Cataloguing in Publication data. A Catalogue record of this book is available from the British Library.

ISBN

978-1-84716-679-1

Printed by 4 Edge www.4edge.co.uk

Contents

OWNER OCCUPIERS AND THE LAW

GENERAL

INTRODUCTION

This revised edition of A Guide to Housing Law, 2017, is a comprehensive overview of housing across three main tenures, Private sector tenants, Public sector tenants and Owner occupiers. There is also a general section covering park homes, houseboats and agricultural tenants.

Housing is very complex and affects all people at some point in their lives. Housing law is ever changing and knowledge of it is usually outside the scope of the layperson. There is the increasing problem of homelessness and what to do at this traumatic time. How do local authorities work and what are their obligations towards the individual? What is the role of housing associations and housing co-operatives and how can one gain access to this type of property, particularly now with the government intent on reducing the availability of social housing?

In addition, what happens if a person is subject to domestic violence and flees home? What are the obligations of local authorities and housing associations at this time? What happens if a relationship breaks down, what are the rights and obligations of the respective parties at a time like this?

A Guide to Housing Law covers the main areas in relation to housing. However, rather than setting out the law in a very dry way, as many housing law tomes tend to do, the book takes the approach of a general advice guide but also at the same time lays out relevant cases dealing with the area in question, at the end of each chapter.

In this way the book should be suitable for both the person generally interested in their rights and also the student or professional.

The law is up to date to 2017.

Roger Sproston

1

HOUSING IN CONTEXT-GENERAL CONSIDERATIONS

Whether to rent or buy

Residential property in the United Kingdom is divided into three broad sectors, owner occupation, private renting and the public sector. the latter is becoming very scarce indeed.

Currently, buying a home in many areas is still only an option for those who can afford the prices. find a deposit and get a mortgage. We are in a market where the majority of first time buyers are still excluded from buying a home. The pattern changes as you move from the south-east to the Midlands and the North, with getting on to the housing ladder still a possibility.

There are distinct advantages to buying a property, if you can. They are as follows:

- When buying you will have a wider choice of property and areas, obviously depending on the price range you can afford.
- You will have more control over your home than when renting.
- You can only normally lose your home if you do not keep up your mortgage repayments.
- In the longer term, it can be cheaper than renting and over the years you will build up equity in the property until you eventually own it.

There are disadvantages to owning, as follows:

- The costs in the early years are usually higher than renting a property, particularly from a local authority or housing association, although usually lower than the private sector.
- There is an initial high cost to buying a house, whereas this is not the case with rented property.
- As an owner-occupier you will be responsible for all repairs and maintenance which can be expensive.
- There is very limited help with your housing costs if your income drops.
- Obviously, the ideal landlord from whom to rent is a local authority or a housing association. **The advantages of this are:**
- Costs are usually lower than the private sector and rents are regulated. However, rents are steadily climbing in the public sector. If your income drops you are usually eligible for housing benefit although there have been significant changes to benefit entitlement in the last few years. Most of the repairs and maintenance will be carried out by the landlord, from rental income.
- You will only lose your home if you breach the terms of the tenancy agreement.
- The public sector is non-profit making and will usually be good landlords.

There are disadvantages to renting from a local authority or housing association:

- In many areas now there is a very long waiting list for properties. When and if you eventually are housed it may not be in an area of choice.
- The rent will gradually increase, reaching levels higher than those who own and you will not build up any equity in your property.

With the advent of buy-to-let, private landlords have increased greatly over the last 25 years, and have become the dominant sector following the credit crunch of 2007,. There are some advantages to renting from a private landlord. They are:

- There will be a wider choice of areas and properties than in the public sector, if you have the means to rent them.
- There is rarely a waiting list.
- You can get help with your rent if your income drops. Most of the repairs and maintenance will be met by the landlord out of rent.

There are, as always, disadvantages to renting in the private sector:

- Rents can be very high. This is the case particularly in the south east.
- Rent will go up over time, usually more than the public sector.
- Tenants in the private sector have limited protection. In the public sector, tenancies are usually for life, subject to breach of contract. Private sector tenants are in the weakest position, with six-month tenancies being the norm.
- Private sector landlords are often poor landlords with scant knowledge of the law.

Different types of house and tenancy will suit different people at different times of their lives, depending on their circumstances. There are many things to consider when making a decision, these being outlined below.

Renting from a local authority

Council homes are, along with housing association property and, in some cases, housing co-operatives, the most affordable type of housing. However, they are also the most difficult to obtain, particularly as there has been a move to make it more difficult for the public sector to build affordable housing. .

The allocation of council housing will depend on your need and those in the most need will usually be given priority over others. This has been a bone of contention for many years, however, as need is measured in a scientific way, with points allocated according to different circumstances. Most local authorities run a bidding system which has made it more difficult for people to both obtain or swap housing.

You can find out from the council housing department about how to go about making an application for housing. If you are being actively considered for an offer of housing then the council will usually send someone to visit you. In most cases, it is necessary to reregister on the housing register each year, in order to keep an active list of those in need.

The housing register

Councils will keep a list, or register of people who apply for housing. This has been a requirement for some years now. This register is also sometimes known as a 'waiting list' although this is misleading since length of time on the list is certainly not the only factor taken into account when it comes to being rehoused. In the main, councils now operate a list where people bid for housing in an area.

A council can decide that a person is not eligible for housing if they have been guilty of behaviour that would entitle them to evict that person as a council tenant.

People arriving from abroad

Some people from abroad are not allowed to register on the housing list. This includes people who are subject to immigration control, people who are allowed to stay subject to not benefiting from public funds and sponsored immigrants who have been in the United Kingdom for less than five years. Also, people who fail the habitual residence test for welfare benefits or who are in breach of EU Rights of Residence Directive. If a local authority refuses to put your name on the housing register, you have the right to ask them to review their decision within 21 days. There are special arrangements for asylum seekers who will be directed towards accommodation in limited areas of the country.

Homelessness

Local authorities have a legal duty to provide help to certain people who are homeless or threatened with homelessness. You will qualify for help if you are 'eligible for assistance', legally homeless or threatened with homelessness and not intentionally homeless. In England, Wales and Northern Ireland, you must also be in priority need. This test was abolished in Scotland on 31 December 2012. The local authority may also investigate whether you have a local connection with the area.

Local social services authorities also have responsibility for some homeless people. They have a duty to provide accommodation for children and young people over 16 who are leaving care, or who are in need for other reasons.

Local authorities must not discriminate against you. For example, if you don't understand English, the local authority should provide help and information in your own language

Eligible for Assistance

Certain people who arrive in this country, or who are returning from a period living abroad do not qualify for housing under homelessness laws. For example, many asylum-seekers (but not all) are excluded, as is someone who has spent significant time living away from the UK even if they are a UK citizen.

The rules on eligibility are complex and if you are arriving in or returning to the UK, you should seek specialist advice at, for example, at a Citizens Advice Bureau.

Homelessness or threatened with homelessness

You will be considered legally homeless if you have no accommodation which is available and reasonable for you and your household to live in. This includes accommodation in another country. You will also be homeless if you have accommodation but cannot get into it. For example, if you have somewhere to stay with friends or relatives but have been asked to leave, or you are at risk of violence in your home. You will be considered to be threatened with homelessness, if you are likely to be homeless within 28 days (in Scotland, two months).

Priority need

You will be counted as having a 'priority need' for housing if you are homeless and:

- you are pregnant

- you have dependent children under 16, or under 19 if they are in full-time education
- you are homeless because of an emergency such as a flood or a fire
- you are aged 16 or 17.

You may also be in priority need if you fall into one of the following groups. In some cases, you may have to show that your situation has made you vulnerable:-

- you are elderly, or have a physical or mental illness or disability
- you are over 18 but at risk of exploitation or have been in care
- you are at risk of domestic violence, racial violence or other threats of violence
- you are homeless after leaving hospital, prison or the armed forces.

The groups of people who have a priority need are different depending on whether you live in England, Wales or Northern Ireland, or in Scotland before the test was abolished.. If you think you fall into a priority need group you can check this with a specialist adviser, for example, at a Citizens Advice Bureau.

Intentionally homeless

You may be considered 'intentionally homeless' if you have deliberately done something which has made you lose your home. However, the definition of intentionally homeless is complicated and a decision made by your local authority can often be successfully challenged. For example, if you have become homeless because of rent or mortgage arrears you should not automatically be considered to be intentionally homeless. The local authority must look at each case individually. If you lost your home because of genuine financial problems you will not be homeless through your own fault.

Priority need

The local authority may refuse to accept responsibility if it thinks that you have no connection with the area where you are looking for help with housing. You would usually be expected to live, work or have family links to have a local connection. In this situation, you may be referred to an area where you do have a connection.

What action must the local authority take?

If the local authority needs time to carry out enquiries (and if it seems that you are homeless and, in England, Wales and Northern Ireland, in priority need), it must make sure you have somewhere to live while it investigates your situation.

If you qualify as homeless, the local authority will have to help you. It does not have to provide accommodation from its own properties. It can house you in various ways, for example, by referring you to a housing association, or arranging accommodation with a private landlord.

If the local authority decides that you are not homeless, it does not have any duties to arrange long-term accommodation for you. However, it will have some duties to help you, and must provide advice and assistance in finding accommodation, or provide a temporary place to stay while you find a permanent home.

The local authority must give reasons for its decision if it decides you aren't homeless and tell you about the right to review a decision, or appeal it, if you live in Northern Ireland.

Other rights to re-housing

People who lose their homes as a result of action by the local authority will, usually, have a right to re-housing. Councils may make a compulsory purchase order on a house and then demolish it, councils may decide that a property needs improving and occupiers have to move out permanently. If this is the case then there is a right to re-housing. Anyone legally living in the property at the time of these actions is entitled to re-housing, the right applying to owners or tenants. It does not apply to those moving in after the action has commenced or to squatters.

People who have to vacate their homes in these circumstances can also claim home loss payment to a maximum of £15,000, (check current figures with your local authority as they are subject to change) disturbance payment to help with the costs of moving and a well-maintained payment which involves a payment to the owners or tenants if the property is to be compulsory purchased and has been well maintained up to the time of compulsory purchase.

Other council housing schemes in operation

In addition to those schemes outlined above, councils have a number of other schemes in operation. The most common are Hard-to-let or low-demand schemes. This is where the council has unpopular homes in areas that are blighted for example, or in tower blocks. Property like this is typically offered to low priority groups such as young single people. However, hard to let schemes in London are almost impossible to find in 2017.

Schemes for special groups-Some council's have quotas for special groups, such as for those with special needs, mental illness etc.

Exchanging properties

Tenants of public sector housing, at least secure and assured tenants, have the right to exchange their homes with another person or family, subject to permission from the landlord, which cannot be unreasonably withheld. There are a number of reasons why the council or association can refuse to let an exchange go ahead:

- There is a court order to evict one of the applicants
- There is impending possession proceedings
- The accommodation you want to transfer is larger than your needs (substantially larger)
- The accommodation is too small
- The landlord is a charity and the proposed new tenant does not suit the aims and objectives of the landlord
- Accommodation is specially adapted for a person with physical disabilities and the proposed new tenant is not disabled.
- The accommodation is managed by a tenant management co-operative and the proposed tenant does not want to become part of the co-operative.

Housing associations

Housing associations and housing trusts are slightly different to councils in their make up. Although publicly funded and accountable to a board of management and to the Homes and Communities Agency (HCA), which regulates the activities of associations, they are more independent than councils.

Housing associations will offer a variety of tenancy types, some not offered by councils. However, they will work closely with the local authority when it comes to receiving nominations and referrals for housing. Often, they are only permitted to develop in a local authority area if they agree an ongoing quota of nominations from councils. Many associations will only house those on the housing register. However, if you have a problem getting onto the housing register then you should seek advice form the council.

Housing associations which are registered with the HCA are obliged by law to give details of how they allocate tenancies. Some associations will take direct applications others will work through agencies. It depends on the associations.

Housing association tenancies are usually assured and assured shorthold, with some secure, usually created out of an exchange. However, as we will see a little later, housing associations have not been able to grant secure tenancies since January 1st 1989 and therefore, the secure tenancy, which is now a local authority tenancy only, is dwindling in associations.

Renting from a private landlord

If you cannot afford to buy a property, as a lot of people cannot due to rising house prices, and you do not qualify for a council or housing association tenancy then you will need to do as a growing number of people do, and that is rent from a private landlord. This is usually the most expensive way of renting but there is usually availability of property.

The majority of private lets are found through local estate agents with a letting arm. They will advertise property and vet prospective tenants, taking up references and also provide a management service to the landlord that can cost anything between 10-15% of rental income plus VAT. Many agencies will charge the tenant a fee for drawing up a tenancy but are not allowed to charge a deposit before a property is found. However, the government has announced that in 2017 lettings agents will be barred from charging tenants fees. On finding a property you will need to pay a deposit which is returnable. The deposit is now protected by the Tenancy Deposit Protection Scheme, introduced in 2007. Renting a property is outlined in more depth further on in the book.

Housing co-operatives

Housing co-operatives consist of groups of people who each have a share in the overall co-op, usually a £1 share and each have a responsibility for managing the co-op, usually delegated to a committee. Individuals are expected to show an active interest and participate in the day-to-day running. Co-ops will allocate their own property but will also sometimes have agreements with local authorities. Three are relatively few co-ops in existence and they are difficult to get into.

****

2

LANDLORD AND TENANT AND THE LAW GENERALLY

Having looked at the housing market, and the main players generally, it is now necessary to outline the fundamentals of the law as it applies to landlord and tenant.

Explaining the law

It is very important for both landlords and tenants to understand the rights and obligations of respective parties to a tenancy and exactly what can and what cannot be done once the tenancy agreement has been signed and the property is occupied.

Some landlords think they can do exactly as they please, because the property belongs to them. Some tenants do not know any differently and therefore the landlord can, and often does, get away with breaking the law. However, this is not the case, there is a very strong legal framework governing the relationship between landlord and tenant and it is important that both parties have a grasp on the key principles of the law.

In order to fully understand the law we should begin by looking at the main types of relationship between people and their homes.

The freehold and the lease

In law, there are two main types of ownership and occupation of property. These are: freehold and leasehold. These arrangements are very old indeed.

Freehold

If a person owns their property outright (usually with a mortgage) then they are a freeholder. The only claims to ownership over and above their own might be those of the building society or the bank, which lent them the money to buy the place. They will re-possess the property if the mortgage payments are not kept up with. In addition, the Crown can exercise rights in times of war, for example.

In certain situations though, the local authority (council) for an area can affect a person's right to do what they please with their home even if they are a freeholder. This will occur when planning powers are exercised, for example, in order to prevent the carrying out of alterations without consent.

The local authority for your area has many powers and we will be referring to these regularly.

Leasehold

If a person lives in a property owned by someone else and has a written agreement allowing them to occupy the flat or house for a period of time i.e., giving them permission to live in that property, then they will, in the main, have a lease and either be a leaseholder or a tenant of a landlord.

The main principle of a lease is that a person has been given permission by someone else to live in his or her property for a period of time. The person giving permission could be either the freeholder or another leaseholder.

The tenancy agreement is one type of lease. If you have signed a tenancy agreement then you will have been given permission by a person to live in their property for a period of time.

The position of the tenant

The tenant will usually have an agreement for a shorter period of time than the typical leaseholder. Whereas the leaseholder will, for example, have an agreement for ninety-nine years, the tenant will have an agreement, which either runs from week to week or month to month (periodic tenancy) or is for a fixed term, for example, six-months or one-year. These arrangements are the most common types of agreement between the private landlord and tenant. The agreement itself will state whether it is a fixed-term or periodic tenancy. If an agreement has not been issued it will be assumed to be a fixed term tenancy. Both periodic and fixed-term tenants will usually pay a sum of rent regularly to a landlord in return for permission to live in the property (more about rent and service charges later)

The tenancy agreement

The tenancy agreement is the usual arrangement under which one person will live in a property owned by another. Before a tenant moves into a property he/she will have to sign a tenancy agreement drawn up by a landlord or landlord's agent. *A tenancy agreement is a contract between landlord and tenant.* It is important to realize that when you sign a tenancy agreement, you have signed a contract with another person, which governs the way in which you will live in their property.

The contract

Typically, any tenancy agreement will show the name and address of the landlord and will state the names of the tenant(s). The type of tenancy agreement that is signed should be clearly indicated. This could be, for example, a Rent Act protected tenancy, an assured tenancy or an assured shorthold tenancy. In the main, in the private sector, the agreement will be an assured shorthold.

Date of commencement of tenancy and rent payable

The date the tenancy began and the duration (fixed term or periodic) plus the amount of rent payable should be clearly shown, along with who is responsible for any other charges, such as water rates, council tax etc, and a description of the property you are living in.

The landlord must also serve a notice stating the address to where any legal notices can be sent. In addition to the rent that must be paid there should be a clear indication of when a rent increase can be expected. This information is sometimes shown in other conditions of tenancy, which should be given to the tenant when they move into their home. The conditions of tenancy will set out landlords and tenants rights and obligations.

Services provided under the tenancy and service of notice

If services are provided, i.e., if a service charge is payable, this should be indicated in the agreement. The tenancy agreement, as stated, should indicate clearly the address to which notices on the landlord can be served by the tenant, for example, because of repair problems or notice of leaving the property. The landlord has a legal requirement to indicate this.

Tenants obligations

The tenancy agreement will either be a basic document with the above information or will be more comprehensive. Either way, there will be a section beginning "the tenant agrees." Here the tenant will agree to move into the property, pay rent, use the property as an only home, not cause a nuisance to others, take responsibility for certain internal repairs, not sublet the property, i.e., create another tenancy, and various other things depending on the property.

Landlords obligations

There should also be another section "the landlord agrees". Here, the landlord is contracting with the tenant to allow quiet enjoyment of the property. The landlord's repairing responsibilities are also usually outlined.

Ending a tenancy through a ground for possession

Finally, there should be a section entitled "ending the tenancy" which will outline the ways in which landlord and tenant can end the agreement. If it is an assured shorthold tenancy then a S21 notice will be served (more about this later). However, it is in this section that the landlord should make reference to the "grounds for possession". Grounds for possession are circumstances where the landlord will apply to court for possession of his/her property. Some of these grounds relate to what is in the tenancy, i.e., the responsibility to pay rent and to not cause a nuisance. Other grounds do not relate to the contents of the tenancy directly, but more to the law governing that particular tenancy. The grounds for possession are very important, as they are used in any court case brought against the tenant. Unfortunately, they are not always indicated in the tenancy agreement. As they are so important they are summarized later on in this chapter.

It must be said at this point that many residential tenancies are very light on landlord's responsibilities. Repairing responsibilities, and responsibilities relating to rental payment, are landlord's obligations under law. This book deals with these, and other areas. However, many landlords will seek to use only the most basic document in order to conceal legal obligations.

The public sector tenancy (local authority or housing association), for example, is usually very clear and very comprehensive about the rights and obligations of landlord and tenant. Unfortunately, the private landlord often does not employ the same energy when it comes to educating and informing the tenant.

Overcrowding /too many people living in the property

It is important to understand, when signing a tenancy agreement, that it is not permitted to allow the premises to become overcrowded, i.e., to allow more people than was originally intended, (which is outlined in the agreement) to live in the property. If a tenant does, then the landlord can take action to evict.

By the same token, landlords are faced with new regulations in 2017 to ensure that they do not create overcrowding. Rogue landlords will be banned from cramming tenants into tiny box rooms in a government initiative to improve housing standards. Rooms must be no smaller than 70sq ft for a single person and 110sq ft for couples, under new rules announced by the Department for Communities and Local Government.

The crackdown comes after an investigation by a newspaper last year found rogue landlords converting two or three bedroom terraced homes into bedsits that house eight or more strangers, each paying £400 to £500 a month for a room. Animal infestations are common and many of the homes have unsafe electrics and are damp. Fire precautions are mostly non-existent. Such overcrowding has caused tensions within communities with neigbours complaining of noise and anti-social behaviour and rubbish over-flowing from small front yards.

Councils will be able to use revenue from the licence fee to enforce the higher standards, with fines of up to £30,000 for the worst offenders.

Different types of tenancy agreement
The protected tenancy - the meaning of the term
As a basic guide, if a person is a private tenant and signed their current

agreement with a landlord before 15th January 1989 then they will, in most cases, be a protected tenant with all the rights relating to protection of tenure, which are considerable. Protection is provided under the 1977 Rent Act. In practice, there are not many protected tenancies left and the tenant will usually be signing an assured shorthold tenancy.

The assured shorthold tenancy - what it means
If the tenant entered into an agreement with a landlord after 15th January 1989 then they will, in most cases, be an assured tenant. We will discuss assured tenancies in more depth in the next chapter In brief, there are various types of assured tenancy. The assured shorthold is usually a fixed term version of the assured tenancy and enables the landlord to recover their property after six months and to vary the rent after this time.

At this point it is important to understand that the main difference between the two types of tenancy, protected and assured, is that the tenant has less rights as a tenant under the assured tenancy. For example, they will not be entitled, as is a protected tenant, to a fair rent set by a Rent Officer.

Other types of agreement
In addition to the above tenancy agreements, there are other types of agreement sometimes used in privately rented property. One of these is the company let, as we discussed in the last chapter, and another is the license agreement. The person signing such an agreement is called a licensee.

Licenses will only apply in special circumstances where the licensee cannot be given sole occupation of his home and therefore can only stay for a short period with minimum rights. There is one other type of agreement is not widely used and that is the Common law tenancy.

Common Law Tenancies

These are tenancies that fall outside the scope of the Housing Acts (1988, 1996, 2004), including the Regulated Tenancies, Assured Tenancies (AT) and Assured Shorthold Tenancies ASTs.

In the case of common law tenancies, the tenant's rights and obligations are mainly dependent on the terms agreed between the parties (written into the agreement), and therefore similar to a commercial lease; they are contractual or "non-statutory contractual tenancies" as opposed to those being regulated by statute.

Commercial (business tenancies) are similar, but businesses have the added protection of the Landlord and Tenant Act 1954, which affords some security of tenure (succession rights) for a businesses on renewal – when the fixed term comes to an end.

Any residential tenancy where the rent equates to an **annual rate in excess of £100,000 pa** (previously £25,000 set in 1990 and increased in October 2010) is excluded from the Housing Act Tenancy (AT or AST) rules and therefore must be a common law tenancy.

Alternatively, where a limited company rents a residential property (usually for their employees) the tenancy will fall outside the scope of the Housing Acts – again it's a common law tenancy.

Often, companies rent residential accommodation and let the property to their employees, usually under a licence agreement (as opposed to a tenancy). Often the employee pays rent and other costs to the landlord, but ultimately the company is liable.

Joint Tenancies and The Common Law Tenancy

A rental rate of £100,000 pa may seem quite a lot, but this also applies to join tenancies where the combined rent of all the sharers (such as students) is included in this total - £8333.33 per month is the limit.

Implications for Landlords – Common Law Tenancies

The implications of common law tenancies are:

(1) a different tenancy agreement from the usual AST will be required, and (2) any deposit taken is not subject to the requirements of the Deposit Protection Scheme under the Housing Act 2004.

(3) the rules governing re-possession under the Housing Acts do not apply.

Security of Tenure – Common Law Tenancies

Common Law Tenancies do not afford tenants the same protection regarding security of tenure and statutory continuation as do Assured Tenancies (including Shorthold Assured Tenancies).

Therefore the AST section 21 and section 8 notices and possession procedures do not apply, and the letting operates on the literal wording of the Tenancy Agreement. Similarly, the Deposit Protection (DPS Scheme) rules do not apply. However, the Protection from Eviction Act 1977 still applies, meaning that in the case of a common law residential tenant refusing to leave, a court order will be required.

Bringing a Common Law Tenancy to an End

With a Common Law tenancy the landlord is entitled to possession at the end of the fixed-term. In theory the landlord is not required to serve a notice to quit to bring the tenancy to an end as the tenancy ends at the agreed date, but in practice the landlord should serve a notice if he wishes the tenant to vacate.

Also, if there are problems during the tenancy, the landlord can bring the common law tenancy to an end where there has been a breach of any of the specified terms in the tenancy agreement. He is not restricted to the prescribed terms (grounds) laid down in Housing Acts.

Statutory Protection for Common Law Tenants

A residential common law tenant still has some statutory protection in that they cannot be evicted against their will unless the landlord obtains a court order (Protection from Eviction Act 1977).

Common Law Tenants will also get protection under the Unfair Terms in Consumer Contracts Regulations 1999, where they have entered into a standard form (pre-printed) tenancy agreement.

They will also benefit from some other statutory provisions including the landlord's repairing obligations under the Landlord and Tenant Act 1985.

Common Law Tenancy Agrements

Landlords or Agents letting to high-rent tenants (above £100,000) or company residential tenants should use the correct type of agreement and not the more common Assured Shorthold Tenancy (AST) ones. All types of letting agreements can be obtained through reputable suppliers they should be custom prepared by an experienced property solicitor.

Squatting

Under section 144 of the Legal Aid, Sentencing and Punishment of Offenders Act, which came into force on the first day of September 2012, squatting in residential buildings (like a house or flat) is illegal. It can lead to 6 months in prison, a £5,000 fine, or both. Squatting is when someone knowingly enters a residential building as a trespasser and lives there, or intends to live there.

A tenant who enters a property with the permission of the landlord, but who falls behind with rent payments, is **not** a squatter. Although squatting a non-residential building or land isn't in itself a crime, trespassers on non-residential property may be committing other crimes.

It's normally a crime for a person to enter private property without permission and refuse to leave when the owner asks. In certain circumstances, it may also be a crime if someone doesn't leave land when they've been directed to do so by the police or council, or if they don't comply with a repossession order.

Squatting in non-residential properties

A non-residential property is any building or land that isn't designed to be lived in.

Simply being on another person's non-residential property without their permission is not usually a crime. But if squatters commit other crimes when entering or staying in a property, the police can take action against them. These crimes could include:

- causing damage when entering the property
- causing damage while in the property
- not leaving when they're told to by a court
- stealing from the property
- using utilities like electricity or gas without permission
- fly-tipping
- not complying with a noise abatement notice

Getting a non-residential property back

If a person owns the property that has been squatted, he or she can use an interim possession order (IPO) to get their property back quickly.

Court action

If the right procedure is followed, they can usually get one issued by the courts within a few days. To get final possession of the property, they must also make an application for possession when they apply for the IPO.

Use form N130 to apply for an interim possession order and for possession.

Exceptions

You can't use an IPO if:

- you're also making a claim for damages caused by the squatters - instead you can make an ordinary claim for possession
- more than 28 days have passed since you found out about the squatters
- you're trying to evict former tenants, sub-tenants or licensees Once squatters are served with an IPO, they must leave the property within 24 hours. If they don't, they're committing a crime and could serve up to 6 months in prison.

It's also a crime for them to return to the property within 12 months.

Squatters taking ownership of a property

It's difficult and very rare for squatters to take ownership of a property. To do this, they would have to stay in a property without the owner's permission for at least 10 years.

****

3
PRIVATE TENANTS-FINDING PROPERTY

....

Letting Agents

One of the first places a prospective private tenant will look to rent a property is a lettings agent. It is important to know what the rules are governing agents as, particularly since the rise in demand for private properties agents have started to use unscrupulous methods to extract more money from tenants and landlords, but particularly tenants,

An amendment to the Enterprise and Regulatory Reform Act 2013 enabled the Government to require agents to sign up to a redress scheme. The Redress Scheme for Lettings Agency Work and Property Management Work (Requirement to Belong to a Scheme etc) (England) Order 2014 made membership of a scheme a legal requirement with effect from 1 October 2014. The Government also amended the Consumer Rights Act 2015 to require letting agents to publish a full tariff of their fees. As mentioned in the previous chapter, it is the governments intention to outlaw the charging of fees by agents in 2017. Until then, If you intend to use an agent to manage your properties or you intend to rent through an agent, then ensure that it is signed up to a redress scheme. One such scheme is The Property Ombudsman Scheme

How do you tell if a letting agent is a TPO registered letting agent?

All agents must display the TPO logo on windows, advertising and stationery. If you need help in finding an agent you can contact the Ombudsman's office or look at the TPO website www.tpos.co.uk.

All agents are required to display copies of the TPO Consumer Guide in their office and make copies available, free of charge, on request.

Online lettings agents

The rise of online lettings agents has been rapid and they now account for 3.5% of the market. The attractions are obvious, the costs. One of the biggest online property agents, EasyProperty.com offers 'pick and mix' services ranging from £10 a week for adverts on Right Move, Prime Location and Zoopla to 3% commission for full property management. For tenant finding with all the frills, such as hosted viewings and professional photos to check-in the total bill would be £445. This equates to less than half the commission charged by high-street agents. Another agent, Purplebricks.com is also very competitive

Typically a (good) letting agent will take responsibility for::

1 Transferring the utility bills and the council tax into the name of the tenant. Sign agreements and take up references.
2 Paying for repairs, although an agent will only normally do this if rent is being paid directly to them and they can make appropriate deductions.
3 Chasing rent arrears.
4 Serving notices of intent to seek possession if the landlord instructs them to do so. An agent cannot commence court proceedings except through a solicitor.
5 Visiting the property at regular intervals and check that the tenants are not causing any damage.
6 Dealing with neighbour complaints.
7 Banking rental receipts if the landlord is abroad

8   Dealing with housing benefit departments if necessary. The extent to which agents actually do any or all of the above really depends on the calibre of the agent. It also depends on the type of agreement you have with the agent.

Immigration Act 2014 and checking eligibility to rent

In October 2014, the new Immigration Act came into force which puts the responsibility on landlords to vet their tenants, or prospective tenants to check to see if they have a right to be in the country. Only when this is verified can a letting go ahead. More information about the checks can be obtained from www.gov.uk.

Company lets

Where the tenant is a company rather than an individual, the tenancy agreement will be similar to an assured shorthold but will not be bound by the six-month rule (see chapter eight for details of assured shorthold tenancies). Company lets can be from any length of time, from a week to several years, or as long as you like.

The major difference between contracts and standard assured shorthold agreements is that the contract will be tailored to individual needs, and the agreement is bound by the provisions of contract law. Company tenancies are bound by the provisions of contract law and not by the Housing Acts.

Short-lets

Generally speaking, short-lets are only applicable in large cities where there is a substantial shifting population. Business executives on temporary relocation, actors and others involved in television production or film work, contract workers and visiting academics are examples of people who might require a short-let.

From a landlord's point of view, short-lets are an excellent idea if they have to vacate your own home for seven or eight months, say, and do not want to leave it empty.

Short-let tenants provide useful extra income as well as keeping an eye on the place. Or if you are buying a new property and have not yet sold the old one, it can make good business sense to let it to a short-let tenant.

Short-let tenants are, usually, from a landlord's point of view, excellent blue-chip occupants. They are busy professionals, high earners, out all day and used to high standards. As the rent is paid by the company there is no worry for the landlord on this score either. A major plus of short-lets is that they command between 20-50 percent more rent than the optimum market rent for that type of property.

The one downside of short-lets is that no agency can guarantee permanent occupancy.

Student lets
Many mainstream letting agencies will not consider students and a lot of landlords similarly are not keen. There is the perception that students will not look after a home and tend to live a lifestyle guaranteed to increase the wear and tear on a property. However, a number of specialist companies have grown up which concentrate solely on students. Although students quite often want property for only eight or nine months, agencies that deal with students make them sign for a whole year. Rent is guaranteed by confirmation that the student is a genuine student with references from parents, who act as guarantors.

Holiday lets
Before the Housing Act 1988 became law, many landlords advertised their properties as holiday lets to bypass the then rules regarding security of

tenure. Strictly speaking, a holiday let is a property let for no more than a month to any one tenant. If the same tenant renews for another month then the landlord is breaking the law. Nowadays, holiday lets must be just that; let for a genuine holiday. If you have a flat or cottage that you wish to let for holiday purposes, whether or not you live in it yourself for part of the year, you are entering into a quite different agreement with the tenant. Holiday lets are not covered by the Housing Act. The contract is finalised by exchange of letters with the tenant where they place a deposit and the owner confirms the booking. If the let is not for a genuine holiday you may have problems in evicting the tenant.

Generally speaking, certain services must be provided for the let to be deemed a holiday let. Cleaning services and changes of bed linen are essential. The amount paid by the holiday-maker will usually include utilities but would exclude use of the telephone, fax machine etc.

Bedsits

Bedsitting rooms are usually difficult to let and can cause problems. There are numerous regulations to adhere to. Houses in Multiple Occupation regulations are quite strict.

The Housing Act 2004 has introduced new tougher regulations for HMOs. If a landlord is letting out property in a block with more than three unrelated dwellings then a licence will be needed from the local authority before lettings can take place.

Landlords taking in a lodger

One way of finding accommodation is to approach people, through websites listed below, who wish to take in a lodger. the following are the main points to consider:

- Under the current Rent a Room Scheme a person can earn rental income of up to £4,250 a year (£354 a month) from a furnished room in their house, without having to pay tax on it. That will change from next April (2017), when the allowance increases to £7,500 a year – or £625 a month

- Prospective Landlords can find lodgers using listings websites such as uk.easyroommate.com and mondaytofriday.com and spareroom.co.uk or fivenights.com (as their names suggest, the last two sites specialise in lodgers who need only weekday accommodation).

- A lodger may be a friend or relation; in other cases, its important to vet anyone thoroughly before they move in. Experian, the credit reference agency, offers a tenants' screening service, under which a landlord can check a prospective tenant's identity, references and ability to pay the rent. The service costs from £15-£25. The prospective tenant must give permission for his or her detail to be shared with you.

- A prospective landlord has certain responsibilities for example, they need to ensure that their gas appliances have been tested for safety. For more details go to gassaferegister.co.uk

- A prospective landlord may prefer to dispense with a legal agreement with your lodger but, if they prefer a more formal relationship they can download the necessary documentation from lawpack.co.uk The agreement should set out every detail of how the arrangement will work, including rent, what parts of the house the lodger can use, whether guests can stay overnight, and on what basis the arrangement can be terminated.

- If the landlord shares their kitchen, bathroom or living room with a lodger, you can evict this person at any time – giving reasonable notice. This is normally 28 days. Under the law, the lodger is viewed as an "excluded occupier" rather than as a tenant. For more on this, see the government website: gov.uk/rent-room-in-your-home/the-rent-a-room-scheme

- A prospective landlord should notify their home and contents insurer and their mortgage lender before taking in a lodger. If they are a tenant themselves, subletting a room in this way could give rise to problems: they should check their own tenancy agreement.

- The Airbnb website enables people to let a room – or whole property – hotel-style, on an ad hoc basis. landlords can charge considerably higher rates per night than they would charge a lodger, and there is greater flexibility as they may choose to let a room for only a few weeks a year. Airbnb hosts with stylish properties in London can charge £150-plus a night for large bedroom with en suite, but guests expect standards commensurate with prices.

- It is free to advertise rooms on airbnb.co.uk. The company sends a photographer to take pictures for your listing. Hosts use the Airbnb site's software to manage bookings, and they pay commission of 3per cent on each accepted reservation. Similar websites include Wimdu. However, Revenue & Customs could consider that regular hosts are running a business, so check before assuming that earnings qualify for the Rent a Room Scheme.

Deposits-Tenancy Deposit Protection Scheme

The Tenancy Deposit Protection Scheme was introduced to protect all deposits paid to landlords after 6th April 2007. After this date, landlords and/or agents must use a government authorised scheme to protect deposits. The need for such a scheme has arisen because of the historical problem with deposits. The scheme works as follows:

Moving into a property

At the beginning of a new tenancy agreement, the tenant will pay a deposit to the landlord or agent as usual. Within 14 days the landlord is required to give the tenant details of how the deposit is going to be protected including:

- the contact details of the tenancy deposit scheme
- the contact details of landlord or agent
- how to apply for the release of the deposit
- what to do if there is a dispute about the deposit

There are three tenancy deposit schemes that a landlord can opt for:
Tenancy Deposit Solutions Ltd
www.mydeposits.co.uk
info@mydeposits.co.uk
The Tenancy Deposit Scheme
www.tds.gb.com
0845 226 7837
The Deposit Protection Service
www.depositprotection.com
0870 707 1 707

The schemes above fall into two categories, insurance based schemes and custodial schemes.

Custodial Scheme

- The tenant pays the deposit to the landlord
- The landlord pays the deposit into the scheme
- Within 14 days of receiving the deposit, the landlord must give the tenant prescribed information
- A the end of the tenancy, if the landlord and tenant have agreed how much of the deposit is to be returned, they will tell the scheme which returns the deposit, divided in the way agreed by the parties.
- If there is a dispute, the scheme will hold the disputed amount until the dispute resolution service or courts decide what is fair
- The interest accrued by deposits in the scheme will be used to pay for the running of the scheme and any surplus will be used to offer interest to the tenant, or landlord if the tenant isn't entitled to it.

Insurance based schemes

- The tenant pays the deposit to the landlord
- The landlord retains the deposit and pays a premium to the insurer (this is the key difference between the two schemes)
- Within 14 days of receiving a deposit the landlord must give the tenant prescribed information.
- At the end of the tenancy if the landlord and tenant agree how the deposit is to be divided or otherwise then the landlord will return the amount agreed

- If there is a dispute, the landlord must hand over the disputed amount to the scheme.

- If for any reason the landlord fails to comply, the insurance arrangements will ensure the return of the deposit to the tenant if they are entitled to it.

If a landlord or agent hasn't protected a deposit with one of the above then the tenant can apply to the local county court for an order for the landlord either to protect the deposit or repay it.

The Deregulation Act 2015

Since 6 April 2007, it has been mandatory for a landlord to ensure that a tenant's deposit that has been paid in respect of an assured shorthold tenancy (AST) is protected within a Tenancy Deposit Scheme. The Deregulation Act now extends the requirement to protect a deposit to AST's created before 6 April 2007 in certain circumstances. Landlords are now required to protect their deposits within a scheme and serve the prescribed information relating to the deposit on the tenant. If a landlord fails to do this then it is prevented from recovering possession of the property from the tenant and is potentially liable for financial penalties.

Rental guarantees

The landlord is always advised to obtain a guarantor if there is any potential uncertainty as to payment of rent. One example is where the tenant is on benefits. The guarantor will be expected to assume responsibility for the rent if the tenant ceases to pay at any time during the term of the tenancy.

****

4

ASSURED TENANTS

Most people, when renting a property through the private sector will become assured tenants, or to be exact assured shorthold tenants, which is a derivation of an assured tenancy. In this chapter we will elaborate on the exact nature of these tenancies.

The assured tenant

As we have seen, with the exception of local authority secure tenancies, (dealt with in chapter   ) and also various other types of agreements, such as company lets, all tenancies, are known as assured tenancies. An assured shorthold, which is the most common form of tenancy used by the private landlord nowadays, is one type of assured tenancy, and is for a fixed term of six months minimum and can be brought to an end with two months notice by serving a section 21 (of the Housing Act 1988) notice (see below) .

It is important to note that all tenancies signed after February 1997 are assured shorthold agreements unless otherwise stated.

Assured tenancies are governed by the 1988 Housing Act, as amended by the 1996 Housing Act. It is to these Acts, or outlines of the Acts that the tenant must refer when intending to sign a tenancy for a residential property.

For a tenancy to be assured, three conditions must be fulfilled:

1. The premises must be a dwelling house. This basically means any premises which can be lived in. Business premises will normally fall outside this interpretation.

2. There must exist a particular relationship between landlord and tenant. In other words there must exist a tenancy agreement. For example, a license to occupy, as in the case of students, or accommodation occupied as a result of work, cannot be seen as a tenancy. Following on from this, the accommodation must be let as a single unit. The tenant, who must be an individual, must normally be able to sleep, cook and eat in the accommodation. Sharing of bathroom facilities will not prevent a tenancy being an assured tenancy but shared cooking or other facilities, such as a living room, will.

3. The third requirement for an assured tenancy is that the tenant must occupy the dwelling as his or her only or principal home. In situations involving joint tenants at least one of them must occupy.

Tenancies that are not assured

A tenancy agreement will not be assured if one of the following conditions applies:

-The tenancy or the contract was entered into before 15th January 1989;
-If no rent is payable or if only a low rent amounting to less than two thirds of the present ratable value of the property is payable;
-If the premises are let for business purposes or for mixed residential and business purposes;
-If part of the dwelling house is licensed for the sale of liquor for consumption on the premises. This does not include the publican who lets out a flat;
-If the dwelling house is let with more than two acres of agricultural land;
-If the dwelling house is part of an agricultural holding and is occupied in relation to carrying out work on the holding;

-If the premises are let by a specified institution to students, i.e., halls of residence;

-If the premises are let for the purpose of a holiday;

-Where there is a resident landlord, e.g., in the case where the landlord has let one of his rooms but continues to live in the house;

-If the landlord is the Crown (the monarchy) or a government department. Certain lettings by the Crown are capable of being assured, such as some lettings by the Crown Estate Commissioners;

-If the landlord is a local authority, a fully mutual housing association (this is where you have to be a shareholder to be a tenant) a newly created Housing Action Trust or any similar body listed in the 1988 Housing Act.

-If the letting is transitional such as a tenancy continuing in its original form until phased out, such as:

-A protected tenancy under the 1977 Rent Act;

-Secure tenancy granted before 1st January 1989, e.g., from a local authority or housing association. These tenancies are governed by the 1985 Housing Act).

The Assured Shorthold tenancy

The assured shorthold tenancy as we have seen, is the most common form of tenancy used in the private sector. The main principle of the assured shorthold tenancy is that it is issued for a period of six months minimum and can be brought to an end by the landlord serving two-months notice on the tenant (Section 21 notice).

New rules for Section 21 notices

If the tenancy started or was renewed on or after 1 October 2015 a landlord will need to use the new prescribed Section 21 notice form (6a).

Section 21 pre-requisites

A landlord cannot serve a valid section 21 notice if:

- They have taken a deposit and not protected and/or served the prescribed information and/or
- They have failed to obtained a license for an HMO property which requires one

If the tenancy was in England and started or was renewed on or after 1 October 2015 a landlord must also have served on their tenant (and you should get proof of service for all these:

- an EPC
- a Gas Safety Certificate, and
- the latest version of the Government's "How to Rent" Guide.

Plus a landlord cannot serve a section 21 notice if their Local Authority has served one of 3 specified notices (the most important being an improvement notice) on them within the past six months in respect of the poor condition of the rental property.

Also, if the tenant complained about the issues covered by the notice prior to this – any Section 21 notice served since the complaint and before the Local Authority notice was served will also be invalid.

The notice period must not be less than two months and must not end before the end of the fixed term (if this has not ended at the time the landlord served their notice)

If this is a periodic tenancy where the period (rent payment period) is more than monthly (e.g., a quarterly or six month periodic tenancy), then the notice period must be at least one full tenancy period.

The notice period does not have to end on a particular day in the month, as was required under the old rules – the landlord just needs to make sure that the notice period is sufficient – minimum of 2 months.

Conditions for an assured shorthold tenancy

Any property let on an assured tenancy can be let on an assured shorthold, providing the following three conditions are met:

- The tenancy must be for a fixed term of not less than six months.
- The agreement cannot contain powers which enable the landlord to end the tenancy before six months. This does not include the right of the landlord to enforce the grounds for possession, which will be approximately the same as those for the assured tenancy
- A notice must be served before any rent increase giving one months clear notice and providing details of the rent increase.

If the landlord wishes to get possession of his/her property, in this case before the expiry of the contractual term, the landlord has to gain a court order. A notice of seeking possession must be served, giving fourteen days notice and following similar grounds of possession as an assured tenancy.
The landlord cannot simply tell a tenant to leave before the end of the agreed term.

If the tenancy runs on after the end of the fixed term then the landlord can regain possession by giving the required two months notice, as mentioned above.

At the end of the term for which the assured shorthold tenancy has been granted, the landlord has an automatic right to possession.

An assured shorthold tenancy will become periodic (will run from week to week) when the initial term of six months has elapsed and the landlord has not brought the tenancy to an end. A periodic tenancy is brought to an end with two months notice. Assured shorthold tenants can be evicted only on certain grounds, some discretionary, some mandatory (see below).

In order for the landlord of an assured shorthold tenant to regain possession of the property, a notice of seeking possession (of property) must be served, giving fourteen days notice of expiry and stating the ground for possession. A copy of this notice is shown in Appendix 2. This notice is similar to a notice to quit, discussed in the previous chapter.

Following the fourteen days a court order must be obtained. Although gaining a court order is not complicated, a solicitor will usually be used. Court costs can be awarded against the tenant.

Security of tenure: The ways in which a tenant can lose their home as an assured shorthold tenant

There are a number of circumstances called grounds (mandatory and discretionary) whereby a landlord can start a court action to evict a tenant.

The following are the *mandatory* grounds (where the judge must give the landlord possession) and *discretionary* grounds (where the judge does not have to give the landlord possession) on which a court can order possession if the home is subject to an assured tenancy.

The mandatory grounds for possession of a property let on an assured (shorthold) tenancy

There are eight mandatory grounds for possession, which, if proved, leave the court with no choice but to make an order for possession. It is very important that you understand these.

Ground One is used where the landlord has served a notice, no later than at the beginning of the tenancy, warning the tenant that this ground may be used against him/her. This ground is used where the landlord wishes to recover the property as his or her principal (first and only) home or the spouse's (wife's or husbands) principal home. *The ground is not available to a person who bought the premises for gain (profit) whilst they were occupied.*

Ground Two is available where the property is subject to a mortgage and if the landlord does not pay the mortgage, could lose the home.

Grounds Three and Four relate to holiday lettings.

Ground Five is a special one, applicable to ministers of religion.

Ground Six relates to the demolition or reconstruction of the property.

Ground Seven applies if a tenant dies and in his will leaves the tenancy to someone else: but the landlord must start proceedings against the new tenant within a year of the death if he wants to evict the new tenant.

Ground Eight concerns rent arrears. This ground applies if, both at the date of the serving of the notice seeking possession and at the date of the hearing of the action, the rent is at least 8 weeks in arrears or two months in arrears. This is the main ground used by landlords when rent is not being paid.

The discretionary grounds for possession of a property, which is let on an assured tenancy

As we have seen, the discretionary grounds for possession are those in relation to which the court has some powers over whether or not the landlord can evict. In other words, the final decision is left to the judge. Often the judge will prefer to grant a suspended order first, unless the circumstances are dramatic.

Ground Nine applies when suitable alternative accommodation is available or will be when the possession order takes effect. As we have seen, if the landlord wishes to obtain possession of his or her property in order to use it for other purposes then suitable alternative accommodation has to be provided.

Ground Ten deals with rent arrears as does *ground eleven*. These grounds are distinct from the mandatory grounds, as there does not have to be a fixed arrear in terms of time scale, e.g., 8 weeks. The judge, therefore, has some choice as to whether or not to evict. In practice, this ground will not be relevant to managers of assured shorthold tenancies.

Ground Twelve concerns any broken obligation of the tenancy. As we have seen with the protected tenancy, there are a number of conditions of the tenancy agreement, such as the requirement not to racially or sexually harass a neighbor. Ground Twelve will be used if these conditions are broken.

Ground Thirteen deals with the deterioration of the dwelling as a result of a tenant's neglect. This is connected with the structure of the property and is the same as for a protected tenancy. It puts the responsibility on the tenant to look after the premises.

Ground Fourteen concerns nuisance, annoyance and illegal or immoral use. This is where a tenant or anyone connected with the tenant has caused a nuisance to neighbors.

Ground 14A this ground deals with domestic violence.

Ground 15 concerns the condition of the furniture and tenants neglect. As Ground thirteen puts some responsibility on the tenant to look after the structure of the building so Ground Fifteen makes the tenant responsible for the furniture and fittings.

Ground 16 covers former employees. The premises were let to a former tenant by a landlord seeking possession and the tenant has ceased to be in that employment.

Ground 17 is where a person or that persons agents makes a false or reckless statement and this has caused the landlord to grant the tenancy under false pretences.

The description of the grounds above is intended as a guide only. A fuller description is contained within the 1988 Housing Act, section 7, Schedule two,) as amended by the 1996 Housing Act) which is available at reference libraries.

Fast track possession

In November 1993, following changes to the County Court Rules, a facility was introduced which enabled landlords of tenants with assured shorthold tenancies to apply for possession of their property without the usual time delay involved in waiting for a court date and attendance at court. This is known as "fast track possession" It cannot be used for rent arrears or other grounds. It is used to gain possession of a property when the fixed term of six months or more has come to an end and the tenant will not move.

Payment of rent

If the landlord wishes to raise rent, at least one month's minimum notice must be given. The rent cannot be raised more than once for the same tenant in one year. Tenants have the right to challenge a rent increase if they think it is unfair by referring the rent to a Rent Assessment Committee. The committee will prevent the landlord from raising the rent above the ordinary market rent for that type of property. We will be discussing rent and rent control further on in this book.

****

5

JOINT TENANCIES

Although it is the normal state of affairs for a tenancy agreement to be granted to one person, this is not always the case.

A tenancy can also be granted to two or more people and is then known as a *joint tenancy*. The position of joint tenants is exactly the same as that of single tenants. In other words, there is still one tenancy even though it is shared. Each tenant is responsible for paying the rent and observing the terms and conditions of the tenancy agreement. No one joint tenant can prevent another joint tenant's access to the premises. If one of the joint tenants dies then his or her interest will automatically pass to the remaining joint tenants. A joint tenant cannot dispose of his or her interest in a will.

Joint tenants usually all have the same rights and responsibilities in their rented home and are all responsible for paying the rent.

Joint Tenancy agreements

You have a joint tenancy if you and your flatmates or housemates all signed a single tenancy agreement with a landlord when you moved in. This means that you all have the same rights and responsibilities. If each of you signed a separate agreement with the landlord, you have separate tenancies.

Rent liability when you're a joint tenant

Joint tenants are all jointly and individually responsible for paying the rent. This means that if one of you moves out without giving notice or is not paying their share, the other joint tenants are responsible for paying it for them. If none of you pay your rent, your landlord can ask any one of you to pay the full amount. All the joint tenants are usually also responsible for paying gas and electricity bills.

Tenancy deposits

When you move into private rented accommodation, you usually need to pay a deposit to cover any damage or unpaid rent. Pay the deposit directly to the landlord or letting agency. If you have an assured shorthold tenancy check that your deposit is put into a tenancy deposit scheme.

Deductions from a tenancy deposit

The landlord normally takes a single deposit for the whole of the tenancy. If one joint tenant fails to pay their share of the rent or if they cause damage to the property, the landlord is entitled to deduct the shortfall or damage from the deposit. You and the other joint tenants decide how to divide up the remaining deposit when it is returned.

Tenancy deposits when a joint tenant moves out

If you are replacing another tenant who is moving out, they may ask you to pay the deposit to them instead. This may not be a good idea. If the tenant who is moving out has caused any damage to the property or left any unpaid bills, the landlord can deduct these costs from the deposit when you move out, which could leave you out of pocket. Get advice if you are in this situation. It might be better to ask the landlord to give a new tenancy agreement to the tenants who is staying on.

Permission for changes

You need to get written permission from the other joint tenants if you want to carry out improvements to the property or pass on or assign your tenancy to someone else.

In most cases you also need your landlord's permission to do any of these things, or if you want to take in a lodger.

Ending a joint tenancy: when one person leaves

The rules on how and when a tenancy can be ended depend on whether the tenancy is fixed-term (for a set period of time) or periodic (rolling from week to week or month to month). See the section on ending a tenancy for more information. If you want to leave, discuss this with the other joint tenants before you take any action.

A fixed-term tenancy cannot be ended early unless all of the joint tenants agree and either:

- your landlord agrees that the tenancy can end early (this is called a 'surrender'), or
- there is a 'break clause' in your tenancy agreement, which allows you to give notice and leave early

If you have a periodic tenancy, or the fixed-term has ended and your tenancy has not been renewed, one tenant can end the whole tenancy and does not need the agreement of the other joint tenants. The landlord must be given a valid written notice and there are special rules about how and when this must be done.

Leaving a joint tenancy

If you want to leave a joint tenancy, it is usually best to discuss it with the other joint tenants before you take any action. If the other joint tenant(s) don't want to move out, they can try to negotiate a new agreement with the landlord. The remaining tenants may be able to find another person to take on the tenancy of the person who wants to leave (the landlord would have to agree to this), or agree with the other joint tenants to stay on and pay the extra rent themselves. Your landlord may decide to:

- give the other tenants a new tenancy agreement, listing the new tenants (in practice, your landlord might not bother to do this)
- accept the rent from the new tenant – in which case the new tenant should have the same rights as a tenant whose name is actually on the tenancy agreement

Eviction of joint tenants

Your landlord cannot evict one joint tenant without evicting all the others. Instead, your landlord may be able to end the tenancy (using the procedures for eviction) and offer a new one to the remaining tenants. Talk to your landlord as soon as possible if you are in this situation and you want to stay.

Relationship breakdown

Get advice if you are worried about losing your home after a relationship breakdown. You may have rights that you are not aware of. For example:

- it may be possible for your joint tenancy to be transferred into one person's name – this can sometimes be done even if the other joint tenant won't agree to it
- it may be possible to stop the other joint tenant from ending the tenancy by applying for an occupation order or an injunction

If you have experienced domestic violence, it may be possible to keep the perpetrator out of your home or to take legal action such as an injunction

Problems with joint tenancies

If you have a problem with another joint tenant you probably have to sort these out yourself. Landlords are usually reluctant to get involved, although council or housing associations are more likely to get involved than private landlords.

****

6

UNDERSTANDING RENT AND OTHER CHARGES

The assured tenant

The assured (shorthold) tenant has far fewer rights in relation to rent control than the protected tenant.

The Housing Act 1988 allows a landlord to charge whatever he likes. There is no right to a fair or reasonable rent with an assured tenancy, which at this moment in time is very high, particularly in London. The rent can sometimes be negotiated at the outset of the tenancy. This rent has to be paid as long as the contractual term of the tenancy lasts. Once the contractual term has expired, the landlord is entitled to continue to charge the same rent.

On expiry of an assured shorthold the landlord is free to grant a new tenancy and set the rent to a level that is compatible with the market.

Rent control for assured shorthold tenants

We have seen that the assured shorthold tenancy is for a period of six months minimum. Like the assured tenant, the assured shorthold tenant has no right to request that a fair rent should be set. The rent is a market rent. As with an assured tenancy, the assured shorthold tenant has the right to appeal to a Rent Assessment Committee in the case of what he/she considers an unreasonable rent.

This may be done during the contractual term. The Committee will consider whether the rent is significantly higher than is usual for a similar property. If the Committee assesses a different rent from that set by the landlord, they may set a date when the increase will take effect. The rent cannot be backdated to before the date of the application. Once a decision has been reached by the Committee, the landlord cannot increase the rent for at least twelve months, or on termination of the tenancy.

Local housing allowance (LHA) (housing benefit) for people who rent a home from a private landlord.

Local housing allowance is housing benefit for private sector tenants. It's usually paid directly to the tenant and they pay their landlord. Local housing allowance is housing benefit that helps pay the rent and some service charges (if applicable) if a person rents from a private landlord. It's a benefit administered by the local council. LHA has many of the same rules as housing benefit, but there are some extra rules that limit the amount of help a tenant can get for a private rented home.

Claim LHA

A person can claim local housing allowance if they are a private tenant who needs help with paying the rent. They may be entitled to this housing benefit if they are working or if they claim benefits.

A person can't get LHA if they have savings of £16,000 or more unless they are a pensioner and receive the guarantee credit part of pension credit. An LHA claim is routinely reassessed after 12 months. The claim may be reassessed at any time if circumstances change.

It is worth noting that, in the July 2015 budget, it was stated that people between the ages of 18-21 will not be entitled to housing benefit in the future. This change has yet to come into effect but you should check with your local authority of you have a prospective tenant between these ages.

How LHA is calculated

The amount of LHA a person can get depends on their income and savings and if any non-dependants live with them, for example adult children.

The amount of LHA they receive also depends on the maximum rent allowed for properties in the area and the number of rooms the council decides a person need.

A person can rent a home of any size or price, but their housing benefit claim is limited. They have to make up any rent shortfall.

Maximum LHA amounts

There are limits on the amount of LHA a person can get. The amount of LHA a person may be eligible for depends on where they live. Local limits are based on the cheapest 30% of properties in an area.

Rooms allowed when calculating LHA

A person is assessed as needing a bedroom for the following people in their home:

- an adult couple
- another person aged 16 or over
- any two children of the same sex up to the age of 16
- any two children regardless of sex under the age of 10
- any other child

New benefit rules which came into effect in April 2013 impose a 'bedroom tax' on tenants and tenants will receive reductions for every bedroom above their needs.

The bedroom tax is a cut in housing benefit if a person lives in a council or housing association home and are classified as having a 'spare' bedroom. The bedroom tax is also known as the under-occupancy charge.

Who the bedroom tax applies to

A person may get less housing benefit if all the following apply:

- They have a spare bedroom
- they live in a council or housing association property
- They of working age

When people reach state pension age they no longer affected. Bedroom tax doesn't apply if a person lives in:

- private rented housing (housing benefit is worked out using different rules)
- temporary or supported accommodation (it does apply to some council facilities)

How much housing benefit a person loses

Bedroom tax is applied to the 'net rent' (the rent when things like water charges are removed, as these aren't covered by housing benefit). This is called 'eligible rent'. The amount of net rent is cut by:

- 14% if a person has one spare bedroom
- 25% two or more spare bedrooms

Bedrooms qualifying for housing benefit

A person can get housing benefit for 1 bedroom for each:
- adult couple
- other adult over 16 (this includes lodgers, although rent from lodgers affects how much housing benefit you get)
- disabled child under 16 who can't share a bedroom because of their disability
- 2 children of the same sex under 16
- 2 children under 10 (including children of the opposite sex)
- foster child (only 1 bedroom is allowed regardless of the number or sex of the children)
- child away at university who plans to return home (second or third year students living in privately rented accommodation may not count)
- child in the armed forces who plans to return home

Any other bedrooms in a home are counted as spare.

Bedrooms a person can't get housing benefit for

A person can't get housing benefit for bedrooms that count as spare bedrooms. This includes rooms used for:

- children who've left home and don't plan to return
- children who live with a person part time and who they don't claim child benefit for
- sleeping apart from a partner because of a medical condition
- a 'sanctuary room', where a home was adapted to make it secure for a person after they experienced domestic violence

When an extra bedroom is allowed

A person can get housing benefit for a bedroom if:

- They disabled and have an overnight carer (only 1 spare bedroom is allowed)
- They are a foster carer who's been approved by social services and is between placements or newly approved (only 1 spare bedroom is allowed for up to 52 weeks)
- They have a child away in the armed or reserve forces (if they plan to return to live with them)
- someone who normally lives with them is away for up to a year if they intend to return and are away for particular reasons (for example, they're in hospital)

Appeals against bedroom tax

In November 2016, the Supreme Court ruled in favour of two bedroom tax appeals from families who argued that they had suffered unlawful discrimination due to their disability and also that the tax affected a person who had been the victim of domestic violence. In the first case, Paul and Susan Rutherford successfully argued that the bedroom tax discriminates against their disabled grandson who requires an overnight carer. In the second case, Jacqueline Carmichael, a severely disabled woman, argued she had been discriminated against after her housing benefit was reduced by

14% because she could not share a bedroom with her husband due to her disability.

It is likely that there will be many other appeals against the bedroom tax, which acioss the board in many cases is draconian, and each case will be decided on its own merit.

If aged under 35

A Person is usually only entitled to LHA at the reduced shared accommodation rate if they are a single person under age 35 without children or they live in shared accommodation.

How often is housing benefit paid?

Payment of housing benefit depends on how often rent is paid. Housing benefit is not paid in advance. Each payment covers a past period.

When LHA can be paid direct to landlords

The council must make a tenant's LHA payments direct to their landlord if:

- they have rent arrears of eight weeks or more
- deductions are being made from benefits for rent arrears
- In some cases, the council can choose to pay LHA direct to the landlord. They could do this if the tenant has failed to pay the rent in the past or have had problems paying rent because of a medical condition. The council can pay LHA direct to a landlord if this will help the tenant keep their tenancy.

If a person has support needs, the council can pay LHA to the landlord to encourage them to keep a person as a tenant.

The council will consult the tenant and people supporting them before deciding to pay LHA direct to the landlord. This may include their doctor, support worker, probation officer and others who know about their situation.

Council tax and the tenant

Council tax is based on properties, or dwellings, and not individual people.

This means that there is one bill for each individual dwelling, rather than separate bills for each person. The number and type of people who live in the dwelling may affect the size of the final bill. A discount of 25 percent is given for people who live alone. Each property is placed in a valuation band with different properties paying more or less depending on their individual value. Tenants who feel that their home has been placed in the wrong valuation band can appeal to their local authority council tax department.

Who has to pay the council tax?

In most cases the tenant occupying the dwelling will have to pay the council tax. That person is known as the 'liable person'. Nobody under the age of 18 can be a liable person.

Couples living together will both be liable even if there is only one name appearing on the bill. However, a landlord will be responsible for paying the council tax where:

- there are several households living in one dwelling where households pay rent separately or;
- where people are under the age of 18;
- the people who live in the property are all asylum seekers who are not entitled to claim benefits including council tax benefits;
- the people who are staying in the property are there temporarily
- or the property is a care home/hospital/hostel or women's refuge.

Although the landlord has the responsibility for paying the council tax, he or she will normally try to pass on the increased cost through rents. However, there is a set procedure for a landlord to follow if he/she wishes to increase rent.

The rules covering council tax liability can be obtained from a Citizens Advice Bureau or from your local authority council tax department.

Service charges-What is a service charge?

A service charge covers a provision of services other than those covered by the rent. In practice, a leaseholder sub-letting his flat will also have to take into account service charges. A rental payment will normally cover maintenance charges, loan charges if any, and also profit. Other services, such as cleaning and gardening, will be covered by a separate charge, known as a service charge. A registered rent reflects the cost of any services provided by the landlord. An assured rent set by a landlord will normally include services which must be outlined in the agreement. The fact that the charges are variable must be written into a tenancy agreement and the landlord has a legal duty to provide the tenant with annual budgets and accounts and has to consult when he or She wishes to spend over a certain amount of money, currently £250 per dwelling for major works such as decorating or £100 if renewing a contract such as gardening, cleaning or lift maintenance, per scheme (estate or block of flats), whichever is the greater.

The form of consultation, which must take place, is that of writing to all those affected informing them of:

- The landlord's intention to carry out work (30 days notice).
- Why these works are seen to be necessary.
- The estimated cost of the works (further 30 days notice).
- At least two estimates or the inviting of them to see two estimates.

The landlord can incur reasonable expense, without consultation, if the work is deemed to be necessary, i.e. emergency works. If a service charge is variable then a landlord has certain legal obligations, which are clearly laid out in the 1985 and 1987 Landlord and Tenant Acts as amended by the 1996 Housing Act and the 2002 Commonhold and Leasehold Reform Act. If you intend to let property for profit then it is of the utmost importance that you understand the law governing service charges.

Payment of housing benefit directly to the landlord

Housing benefit is a payment made to the tenant rather than the landlord. The amount of benefit that a tenant is paid will very much depend on that persons circumstances. The rules regarding payment of housing benefit have tightened considerably over the years and if you know that a tenant is going to be claiming housing benefit then you should be sure that they will be entitled. Local authorities have local rents that they will pay and they will not pay, for example, for a single person to occupy accommodation surplus to their needs or for anyone to claim what they see as excessive rent.

Housing benefit and possession for arrears of rent

Very often, problems in obtaining benefit will cause tenants to accrue rent arrears. The court is unlikely to give possession if arrears are accruing because of benefit.

Once there are eight weeks of arrears (see grounds for possession) then the court has no choice but to give possession anyway and quite often it is better to wait rather than jumping the gun and losing rental income altogether. If on the other hand the tenant has stated that they are going to pay rent personally rather than benefit then the court will look more favorably on- giving possession to the landlord if arrears have arisen as a result of an immediate claim for benefit.

****

7

THE RIGHT TO QUIET ENJOYMENT OF A HOME

Earlier, we saw that when a tenancy agreement is signed, the landlord is contracting to give quiet enjoyment of the tenant's home. This means that they have the right to live peacefully in the home without harassment.

The landlord is obliged not to do anything that will disturb the right to the quiet enjoyment of the home. The most serious breach of this right would be for the landlord to wrongfully evict a tenant.

Eviction: what can be done against unlawful harassment and eviction
It is a criminal offence for a landlord unlawfully to evict a residential occupier (whether or not a tenant!). The occupier has protection under the Protection from Eviction Act 1977 section 1(2).

If the tenant or occupier is unlawfully evicted his/her first course should be to seek an injunction compelling the landlord to readmit him/her to the premises. It is an unfortunate fact but many landlords will attempt to evict tenants forcefully. In doing so they break the law.

However, the landlord may, on termination of the tenancy recover possession without a court order if the agreement was entered into after 15th January 1989 and it falls into one of the following six situations:

- The occupier shares any accommodation with the landlord and the landlord occupies the premises as his or her only or principal home.
- The occupier shares any of the accommodation with a member of the landlords family, that person occupies the premises as their only or principal home, and the landlord occupies as his or her only or principal home premises in the same building.
- The tenancy or license was granted temporarily to an occupier who entered the premises as a trespasser.

- The tenancy or license gives the right to occupy for the purposes of a holiday.
- The tenancy or license is rent-free.
- The license relates to occupation of a hostel.

There is also a section in the 1977 Protection from Eviction Act which provides a defense for otherwise unlawful eviction and that is that the landlord may repossess if it is thought that the tenant no longer lives on the premises. It is important to note that, in order for such action to be seen as a crime under the 1977 Protection from Eviction Act, the intention of the landlord to evict must be proved. However, there is another offence, namely harassment, which also needs to be proved. Even if the landlord is not guilty of permanently depriving a tenant of their home he/she could be guilty of harassment. Such actions as cutting off services, deliberately allowing the premises to fall into a state of disrepair, or even forcing unwanted sexual attentions, all constitute harassment and a breach of the right to *quiet enjoyment.*

The 1977 Protection from Eviction Act also prohibits the use of violence to gain entry to premises. Even in situations where the landlord has the right to gain entry without a court order it is an offence to use violence.

If entry to the premises is opposed then the landlord should gain a court order.

What can be done against unlawful evictions?

There are two main remedies for unlawful eviction: damages and, as stated above, an injunction. An injunction is an order from the court requiring a person to do, or not to do something. In the case of eviction the court can grant an injunction requiring the landlord to allow a tenant back into occupation of the premises. In the case of harassment an order can be made preventing the landlord from harassing the tenant. Failure to comply with an injunction is contempt of court and can result in a fine or imprisonment.

Damages

In some cases the tenant can press for *financial compensation* following unlawful eviction. Financial compensation may have to be paid in cases where financial loss has occurred or in cases where personal hardship alone has occurred.

The tenant can also press for *special damages,* which means that the tenant may recover the definable out-of-pocket expenses. These could be expenses arising as a result of having to stay in a hotel because of the eviction. Receipts must be kept in that case. There are also *general damages,* which can be awarded in compensation for stress, suffering and inconvenience.

A tenant may also seek *exemplary damages* where it can be proved that the landlord has disregarded the law deliberately with the intention of making a profit out of the displacement of the tenant.

****

8

LANDLORD AND TENANT REPAIRING OBLIGATIONS

Repairs and improvements generally: The landlord and tenants obligations

Repairs are essential works to keep the property in good order. Improvements and alterations to the property, e.g. the installation of a shower. (see summary of disrepair cases at the end of the chapter).

As we have seen, most tenancies are periodic, i.e. week-to-week or month-to-month. If a tenancy falls into this category, or is a fixed-term tenancy for less than seven years, and began after October 1961, then a landlord is legally responsible for most major repairs to the flat or house.

If a tenancy began after 15th January 1989 then, in addition to the above responsibility, the landlord is also responsible for repairs to common parts and service fittings.

The area of law dealing with the landlord and tenants repairing obligations is the 1985 Landlord and Tenant Act, section 11.

This section of the Act is known as a covenant and cannot be excluded by informal agreement between landlord and tenant. In other words the landlord is legally responsible whether he or she likes it or not. Parties to a tenancy, however, may make an application to a court mutually to vary or exclude this section.

Example of repairs a landlord is responsible for:
- Leaking roofs and guttering.
- Rotting windows.
- Rising damp.
- Damp walls.

- Faulty electrical wiring.
- Dangerous ceilings and staircases.
- Faulty gas and water pipes.
- Broken water heaters and boilers.
- Broken lavatories, sinks or baths.

In shared housing the landlord must see that shared halls, stairways, kitchens and bathrooms are maintained and kept clean and lit.

Normally, tenants are responsible only for minor repairs, e.g., broken door handles, cupboard doors, etc. Tenants will also be responsible for decorations unless they have been damaged as a result of the landlord's failure to do repair.

A landlord will be responsible for repairs only if the repair has been reported. It is therefore important to report repairs in writing and keep a copy. If the repair is not carried out then action can be taken. Damages can also be claimed.

Compensation can be claimed, with the appropriate amount being the reduction in the value of the premises to the tenant caused by the landlord's failure to repair. If the tenant carries out the repairs then the amount expended will represent the decrease in value.

The tenant does not have the right to withhold rent because of a breach of repairing covenant by the landlord. However, depending on the repair, the landlord will not have a very strong case in court if rent is withheld.

Reporting repairs to landlords

The tenant has to tell the landlord or the person collecting the rent straight away when a repair needs doing. It is advisable that it is in writing, listing the repairs that need to be done.

Once a tenant has reported a repair the landlord must do it within a reasonable period of time. What is reasonable will depend on the nature of the repair.

The tenants rights whilst repairs are being carried out

The landlord must ensure that the repairs are done in an orderly and efficient way with minimum inconvenience to the tenant If the works are disruptive or if property or decorations are damaged the tenant can apply to the court for compensation or, if necessary, for an order to make the landlord behave reasonably.

If the landlord genuinely needs the house empty to do the work he/she can ask the tenant to vacate it and can if necessary get a court order against the tenant.

A written agreement should be drawn up making it clear that the tenant can move back in when the repairs are completed and stating what the arrangements for fuel charges and rent are.

Can the landlord put the rent up after doing repairs?

If there is a service charge for maintenance, the landlord may be able to pass on the cost of the work(s).

Tenants rights to make improvements to a property

Unlike carrying out repairs the tenant will not normally have the right to insist that the landlord make actual alterations to the home. However, a tenant needs the following amenities and the law states that you should have:

- Bath or shower.
- Wash hand basin.
- Hot and cold water at each bath, basin or shower.
- An indoor toilet.

If these amenities do not exist then the tenant can contact the council's Environmental Health Officer. An improvement notice can be served on the landlord ordering him to put the amenity in.

Disabled tenants

If a tenant is disabled he/she may need special items of equipment in the accommodation. The local authority may help in providing and, occasionally, paying for these. The tenant will need to obtain the permission of the landlord. If you require more information then contact the social services department locally.

Shared housing. The position of tenants in shared houses (Houses in Multiple Occupation)

A major change to improve standards of shared housing was introduced in 2006. The parts of the Housing Act 2004 relating to the licensing of HMO's (Houses in Multiple Occupation) and the new Health and Safety Rating System for assessing property conditions came into effect on 6rh April 2006.

The Act requires landlords of many HMO's to apply for licences. The HMO's that need to be licensed are those with:

- Three or more storeys, which are
- Occupied by five or more people forming two or more households (i.e. people not related, living together as a couple etc) and
- Which have an element of shared facilities (eg kitchen, bathroom etc)

As far as licensing is concerned, attics and basements are included as storeys if they are used as living accommodation. Previously, HMO's were only defined as houses converted into flats or bedsits, but the new Act widens this definition and many more types of shared houses are now included.

A local authority will have a list of designated properties will have a list of those properties which are designated HMO's and they will need to be licensed.

- Usually, landlords will need to apply to a local authority private sector unit for licences. It is illegal for landlords to manage designated properties without a licence since July 2006. Landlords will have to complete an application form and pay a fee, the local authority will then assess whether the property is suitable for the number of people the landlord wants to rent it to. In most case, the local authority, their agents, will visit a property to assess facilities and also fire precautions. A decision will then be taken to grant a license. There is a fee for registration and councils set the fee which may differ in each area.

The landlord of a HMO has certain duties under the regulations to his/her tenants:

Duty to provide information

The manager (this means that whoever is charged with the management of the building) must ensure that:

- His name, address and telephone number are available to each household in the HMO
- These details are also clearly displayed in a prominent position in the HMO.

The manager should maintain a log book to record all events at the property such as:

- Testing of fire alarms
- Testing of fire fighting equipment
- Gas safety certificate
- Electrical report
- Inspection and wants of repair

Duty to take safety measures

The manager must ensure that all means of escape from fire in the property are kept free from obstruction and in good order as should all fire alarms and equipment.

The manager should ensure that the structure is designed and maintained in a safe condition, and also take steps to protect occupiers from injury. In properties with four or more occupants, the Regulations provide that fire escape notices be clearly displayed.

Duty to maintain water supply drainage

The manager must ensure that the water supply and drainage system serving the property are maintained in a good working condition. More specifically, water fittings should be protected from frost and all water storage tanks should be provided with covers.

Duty to supply and maintain gas and electricity

The manager must supply the local housing authority within 7 days of receiving a written request a safety certificate. The manager must ensure that the fixed electrical installation is checked at least once every three years by a suitably qualified electrician and supply this to the LHA on written request. In addition to the above, there is a duty to maintain common parts, fixtures, fittings and appliances. There is a duty to maintain living accommodation and to provide waste disposal facilities.

Powers of the local authority in relation to HMO's

It is essential to ensure that, if you have invested in a HMO that you manage it rigorously because local authorities have sweeping powers to fine landlords and to revoke licenses. A local authority can prosecute a landlord who does not obtain a license for a HMO.

Safety generally for all landlords-the regulations

The main product safety regulations relevant to the lettings industry are:

Gas safety

The Gas safety (Installation and use) Regulations 1998
The Gas Cooking Appliances (safety) Regulations 1989
Heating Appliances(Fireguard) (safety) Regulations 1991
Gas Appliances(Safety) Regulations 1995

All of the above are based on the fact that the supply of gas and the appliances in a dwelling are safe. A Gas Safety certificate is required to validate this.

Furniture Safety

Furniture and Furnishings (Fire) (Safety) Regulations 1988 and 1993 (as amended). Landlords and lettings agents are included in these regulations. The regulations set high standards for fire resistance for domestic upholstered furniture and other products containing upholstery.

The main provisions are:

- Upholstered articles (i.e. beds, sofas, armchairs etc) must have fire resistant filling material.
- Upholstered articles must have passed a match resistant test or, if of certain kinds (such as cotton or silk) be used with a fire resistant interliner.
- The combination of the cover fabric and the filling material must have passed a cigarette resistance test.

The landlord should inspect property for non-compliant items before letting and replace with compliant items.

Electrical Safety

Electrical Equipment (Safety) Regulations 1994
Plugs and Sockets etc. (Safety) Regulations 1994.

The Electrical Equipment Regulations came into force in January 1995. Both sets of regulations relate to the supply of electrical equipment designed with a working voltage of between 50 and 1000 volts ac. (or between 75 and 1000 volts dc.) the regulations cover all the mains voltage household electrical goods including cookers, kettles, toasters, electric blankets, washing machines, immersion heaters etc. The regulations do not apply to items attached to land. This is generally considered to exclude the fixed wiring and built in appliances (e.g. central heating systems) from the regulations. Lettings agents and landlords should take the following action:

Essential:
Check all electrical appliances in all managed properties on a regular fixed term basis. Remove unsafe items and keep a record of checks.

Recommended:

- Have appliances checked by a qualified electrical engineer
- Avoid purchasing second hand electrical items
- There is no specific requirement for regular testing under the regulations. However, it is recommended that a schedule of checks, say on an annual basis, is put in place.

The availability of grants
There are a number of grants available to landlords at any one time which will enable improvements to take place to a property. One of the main grants is the Disabled facilities Grant. However, there are more and your local authority can tell you what is available.

New regulations on Smoke and Carbon Monoxide detectors
From October 2015, all landlords, regardless of whether public or private sector, will be required to install working smoke and carbon monoxide alarms in their properties, on each floor. The carbon monoxide alarms will

need to be placed in high risk areas, i.e., where there are gas appliances such as boilers or fires. Carbon monoxide detectors will not be required in properties where there are no gas or solid fuel appliances. A civil penalty of up to £5,000 will apply to landlords who fail to comply with this legislation.

Sanitation health and hygiene

Local authorities have a duty to serve an owner with a notice requiring the provision of a WC when a property has insufficient sanitation, sanitation meaning toilet waste disposal.

They will also serve notice if it is thought that the existing sanitation is inadequate and is harmful to health or is a nuisance.

Local authorities have similar powers under various Public Health Acts to require owners to put right bad drains and sewers, also food storage facilities and vermin, plus the containing of disease.

The Environmental Health Department, if it considers the problem bad enough will serve a notice requiring the landlord to put the defect right. In certain cases the local authority can actually do the work and require the landlord to pay for it. This is called work in default.

*

****

9

TAKING BACK POSSESSION OF A PROPERTY

....

Fast-track possession

A landlord cannot serve a s21 notice on an assured shorthold tenant until after the first four months of a tenancy (if it is for a six moth period). This brings the tenancy to an end on the day of expiry, i.e. on the day of expiry of the six month period,

New rules for Section 21 notices

If the tenancy started or was renewed on or after 1 October 2015 a landlord will need to use the new prescribed Section 21 notice form (6a).

Section 21 pre-requisites

A landlord cannot serve a valid section 21 notice if:

- They have taken a deposit and not protected and/or served the prescribed information and/or
- They have failed to obtained a license for an HMO property which requires one

If the tenancy was in England and started or was renewed on or after 1 October 2015 a landlord must also have served on their tenant (and you should get proof of service for all these:

- an EPC
- a Gas Safety Certificate, and
- the latest version of the Government's "How to Rent" Guide.

Plus a landlord cannot serve a section 21 notice if their Local Authority has served one of 3 specified notices (the most important being an improvement notice) on them within the past six months in respect of the poor condition of the rental property.

Also, if the tenant complained about the issues covered by the notice prior to this – any Section 21 notice served since the complaint and before the Local Authority notice was served will also be invalid.

The notice period must not be less than two months and must not end before the end of the fixed term (if this has not ended at the time the landlord served their notice)

If this is a periodic tenancy where the period (rent payment period) is more than monthly (e.g., a quarterly or six month periodic tenancy), then the notice period must be at least one full tenancy period.

The notice period does not have to end on a particular day in the month, as was required under the old rules – the landlord just needs to make sure that the notice period is sufficient – minimum of 2 months.

On expiry of the notice, if it is the landlord's intention to take possession of the property then the tenants should leave. It is worthwhile writing a letter to the tenants one month before expiry reminding them that they should leave.

In the event of the tenant refusing to leave, then the landlord has to then follow a process termed 'fast track possession'. This entails filling in the appropriate forms (N5B) which can be downloaded from Her Majesty's Court Service Website www.justice.gov.uk.

Assuming that a valid section 21 notice has been served on the tenant, the accelerated possession proceedings can begin and the forms completed and lodged with the court dealing with the area where the property is situated. In order to grant the accelerated possession order the court will require the following:

- The assured shorthold agreement
- The section 21 notice
- Evidence of service of the section 21 notice

The best form of service of the s21 notice is by hand. If you have already served the notice then evidence that the tenant has received it will be required.

Having the correct original paperwork is of the utmost importance. Without this, the application will fail and delays will be incurred.

If the tenant disputes the possession proceedings in any way they will have 14 days to reply to the court. If the case is well founded and the paperwork is in order then there should be no case for defence. Once the accelerated possession order has been granted then this will need to be served on the tenant, giving them 14 days to vacate. In certain circumstances, if the tenant pleads hardship the court can grant extra time to leave, six weeks as opposed to two weeks. If they still do not vacate then an application will need to be made to court for a bailiffs warrant to evict the tenants.

Accelerated possession proceedings cannot be used against the tenant for rent arrears. It will be necessary to follow the procedure below.

An accelerated possession order remains in force for six years from the date it was granted.

Going to court to end the tenancy

There may come a time when a landlord needs to go to court to regain possession of their property. This will usually arise when the contract has been breached by the tenant, for non-payment of rent or for some other breach such as nuisance or harassment. As we have seen, a tenancy can be brought to an end in a court on one of the grounds for possession. However, as the tenancy will usually be an assured shorthold then it is necessary to consider for the landlord to consider whether they are in a position to give two months notice and withhold the deposit, as opposed to going to court. The act of withholding the deposit will entail the landlord refusing to authorize the payment to the tenant online. This then brings arbitration into the frame. Deposit schemes have an arbitration system as an integral part of the scheme.

If a landlord decides, for whatever reason, to go to court, then any move to regain a property for breach of agreement will commence in the county court in the area in which the property is. The first steps in ending the tenancy will necessitate the serving of a notice of seeking possession using one of the Grounds for Possession detailed earlier in the book. If the tenancy is protected then 28 days must be given, the notice must be in prescribed form and served on the tenant personally (preferably).

If the tenancy is an assured shorthold, which is more often the case now, then 14 days notice of seeking possession can be used. In all cases the ground to be relied upon must be clearly outlined in the notice. If the case is more complex, then this will entail a particulars of claim being prepared, usually by a solicitor, as opposed to a standard possession form.

A fee is paid when sending the particulars to court, which should be checked with the local county court. The standard form which the landlord uses for routine rent arrears cases is called the N119 and the accompanying summons is called the N5. Both of these forms can be obtained from the court or from www.courtservice.gov. When completed, the forms should be sent in duplicate to the county court and a copy retained for you.

The court will send a copy of the particulars of claim and the summons to the tenant. They will send you a form which gives you a case number and court date to appear, known as the return date. On the return date, you should arrive at court at least 15 minutes early. You can represent yourself in simple cases but are advised to use a solicitor for more contentious cases. When it is your turn to present the case, you should have your file in order, a copy of all relevant notices served and a current rent arrears figure or a copy of the particulars for other cases.

If it is simple rent arrears then quite often the judge will guide you through.

However, the following are the steps to observe:
- State your name and address.
- Tenants name and address.
- Start date of tenancy.
- Current rent and arrears.
- Date notice served-a copy should be produced for the judge.

•Circumstances of tenant (financial and other) this is where you make your case.
•Copy of order wanted.

If the tenant is present then they will have a chance to defend themselves.

A number of orders are available. However, if you have gone to court on the mandatory ground eight then if the fact is proved then you will get possession immediately. If not, then the judge can grant an order, suspended whilst the tenant finds time to pay.

In a lot of cases, it is more expedient for a landlord to serve notice-requiring possession, if the tenancy has reached the end of the period, and then wait two months before the property is regained. This saves the cost and time of going to court particularly if the ground is one of nuisance or other, which will involve solicitors.

In many cases, if you are contemplating going to court and have never been before and do not know the procedure then it is best to use a solicitor to guide the case through.

Costs can be recovered from the tenant, although this will depend on their means. If you regain possession of your property midway through the contractual term then you will have to complete the possession process by use of bailiff, pay a fee and fill in another form, Warrant for Possession of Land.

If you have reached the end of the contractual term and wish to recover your property then a fast track procedure is available which entails gaining an order for possession and bailiff's order by post. This can be used in cases with the exception of rent arrears.

****

10

PRIVATE TENANCIES IN SCOTLAND

The law governing the relationship between private landlords and tenants in Scotland is different to that in England. Since the beginning of 1989, new private sector tenancies in Scotland have been covered by the Housing (Scotland) Act 1988. Following the passage of this Act, private sector tenants no longer have any protection as far as rent levels are concerned and tenants enjoy less security of tenure.

There are four essential elements in the creation of a tenancy under Scottish law:

- An agreement between landlord and tenant
- The payment of rent. If someone is allowed to occupy a property without an agreement then this will not amount to a tenancy
- A fixed permission date (called an 'ish')
- Possession

The agreement must be in writing if the tenancy is for a period of 1 year or more. Agreements of less than a year can be oral.

Protected tenancies

Before 1989, most private sector tenancies were likely to be protected tenancies. A protected tenancy is a contractual tenancy covered by the Rent Act (Scotland) 1984 and must satisfy the following requirements:

- The house must be let as a dwelling house (this can apply to a house or part of a house)
- The house must be a separate dwelling
- The ratable value must be less than a specified sum

Various categories of dwellings did not qualify as protected tenancies. A protected tenancy retains its status until the death of a tenant or his or her spouse, or any eligible successor, and therefore some protected tenancies are still in existence today.

Grounds for possession

As is the case in England and Wales, where there is no protected tenancy, the landlord may possess a property only by obtaining a court order. The landlord must serve a notice to quit, giving 28 days notice. A ground for possession must be shown, either discretionary or mandatory before possession can be given.

The grounds for possession are similar to those in England and Wales, with ten mandatory and ten discretionary grounds applying.

Fair rent system

A fair rent system, similar to England and Wales, exists in Scotland for protected tenants. There is a set procedure to be followed, with either the landlord or tenant, or jointly, making an application to the rent officer. Once fixed, the rent is valid for three years. A fresh application can be made within three years if circumstances relating to the tenancy radically alter, such as a substantial refurbishment.

Assured tenants

Under the Housing (Scotland) Act 1988, the assured tenancy was introduced into Scotland coming into force after 2nd January 1989. This is very similar indeed to the assured tenancy introduced into England and Wales in 1989.

A Scottish assured tenancy has three elements:

- the tenancy must be of a house or flat or self contained dwelling. For an agreement to exist, there must be an agreement, rent payable a termination date and possession, as there is in all leases in Scotland

- The house must be let as a separate dwelling. A tenancy may be of a flat, part of a house, or even a single room, provided it is possible for the tenant to carry on all 'the major activities of residential life there, i.e. sleeping, cooking and feeding'.
- The tenant must be an individual. A company cannot be given an assured tenancy

The list of exclusions from assured tenancy status are the same as those in England and all the other provisions concerning rent, sub-letting succession, security of tenure and so on, apply.

The grounds for possession and the law governing termination of tenancies is a reflection of English Law.

Short assured tenancies

The Housing Act (Scotland) also introduced 'short assured tenancies', a distinct form of assured tenancy for a fixed term of six months. Again, this is a reflection of the assured shorthold with the same provisions applying.

****

PUBLIC SECTOR TENANCIES

11

PUBLIC SECTOR TENANCIES

Renting from a social housing landlord
Who is a tenant of a social housing landlord

You are a tenant of a social housing landlord if you are a tenant of:

- a local authority. These are district councils and London borough councils; or
- a housing association; or
- a housing co-operative.

Local authority tenants
If you are a tenant of a local authority you are likely to be a secure tenant or an introductory tenant. In England, from 1 April 2012, local authorities can also grant flexible tenancies.

Housing association and housing co-operative tenants
Tenancy began before 15 January 1989
If you are a housing association or housing co-operative tenant and your tenancy began before 15 January 1989, you will be a secure tenant. For details about the rights a secure tenant has, see below.

Tenancy began on or after 15 January 1989
If you are a housing association or housing co-operative tenant and your tenancy began on or after 15 January 1989, you are likely to be an assured tenant. Some association tenants may be starter tenants for the first 12 to 18 months. A starter tenancy is a type of assured shorthold tenancy.

In England, from 1 April 2012, housing associations can use assured shorthold tenancies for tenancies other than starter tenancies.

Rights of secure tenants

As a secure tenant you have the right to stay in the accommodation unless your landlord can convince the court that there are special reasons to evict you, for example, you have rent arrears, damaged property or broken some other term of the agreement. As well as the right to stay in your home as long as you keep to the terms of the tenancy, you will also have other rights by law: These include the right:

- to have certain repairs carried out by your landlord
- to carry out certain repairs and to do improvements yourself - see under heading Repairs and improvements
- to sublet part of your home with your landlord's permission
- to take in lodgers without your landlord's permission
- to exchange your home with certain other social housing tenants
- if you are a local authority tenant, the right to vote to transfer to another landlord
- to be kept informed about things relating to your tenancy
- to buy your home.
- if you are a housing association tenant whose tenancy started before 15 January 1989, the right to a 'fair rent' - see under heading Fixing and increasing the rent
- for your spouse, civil partner, other partner or in some cases a resident member of your family, to take over the tenancy on your death (the right of 'succession')
- to assign (pass on) the tenancy to a person who has the right of 'succession' to the tenancy. This is sometimes difficult to enforce
- if you are a local authority tenant, to take over the management of the estate with other tenants by setting up a Tenant Management Organisation

- not to be discriminated against because of your disability, gender reassignment, pregnancy and maternity, race, religion or belief, sex or sexual orientation.

You will usually have a written tenancy agreement which may give you more rights than those set out above.

Complaints about secure tenancies

Each social housing landlord must have a clear policy and procedure on dealing with complaints. You should have the opportunity to complain in a range of ways. If after using your landlord's complaints procedure you are still dissatisfied, you can complain to an Ombudsman about certain problems. In England, if you are a local authority tenant this will be the Local Government Ombudsman, and if you are a housing association tenant it will be the Housing Ombudsman. If you have suffered discrimination, you can complain about this to the Ombudsman. In Wales, you can complain to the Public Services Ombudsman for Wales.

Rights of assured tenants

As an assured tenant you have the right to stay in your accommodation unless your landlord can convince the court there are reasons to evict you, for example, that there are rent arrears, damage to the property, or that another of the terms of the agreement has been broken.

As an assured tenant you can enforce your rights, for example, to get repairs done, without worrying about getting evicted. As well as the right to stay in your home as long as you keep to the terms of the tenancy you will also have other rights by law including:-

- the right to have the accommodation kept in a reasonable state of repair
- the right to carry out minor repairs yourself and to receive payment for these from your landlord - see under heading Repairs and improvements

- the right for your spouse, civil partner or other partner to take over the tenancy on your death (the right of 'succession')
- the right not to be treated unfairly by your landlord because of your disability, gender reassignment, pregnancy and maternity, race, religion or belief, sex or sexuality.

You will usually have a written tenancy agreement which may give you more rights than those set out above.

Complaints about assured tenancies
Each housing association must have a clear policy and procedure on dealing with complaints. You should have the opportunity to complain in a range of ways. If after using your landlord's complaints procedure you are still dissatisfied, you can complain in England, to the Housing Ombudsman, or in Wales, to the Public Services Ombudsman for Wales.

Starter tenancies and assured shorthold tenancies
A starter tenancy is the name often used by housing associations to describe an assured shorthold tenancy. Starter tenancies are probationary tenancies which allow a landlord to evict you more easily if you break the terms of your tenancy agreement.

A starter tenancy generally lasts for 12 months, although they can be extended to 18 months. As long as no action has been taken by the landlord to end the tenancy within the starter period, the starter tenant can then become an assured or longer-term assured shorthold tenant in England, or an assured tenant in Wales.

In England, housing associations can use assured shorthold tenancies for tenancies other than starter tenancies. They are likely to last for a fixed term of five years or more, but in some cases will last for two years. These tenancies may also be on 'affordable rent' terms.

In England, if you have an assured shorthold tenancy of a fixed term of two years or more with a housing association landlord, you will generally have similar rights to an assured tenant. However, if you have a fixed term tenancy, you only have the right to stay in your home for the length of the fixed term.

Complaints about starter and assured shorthold tenancies

Each housing association must have a clear policy and procedure on dealing with complaints. You should have the opportunity to complain in a range of ways. If after using your landlord's complaints procedure you are still dissatisfied, you can complain in England, to the Housing Ombudsman, or in Wales, to the Public Services Ombudsman for Wales.

Fixing and increasing the rent
Secure tenants
Local authority tenancies

Rents for local authority tenants are fixed according to the local authority's housing policy and the amount of money they get from central government. You cannot control the amount of rent payable, but may be able to claim housing benefit to help pay it.

Housing association and housing co-operative tenancies which began before 15 January 1989

If you are a housing association or housing co-operative tenant whose tenancy started before 15 January 1989 you are a secure tenant, but your rent is generally a 'fair rent' registered by the Rent Officer. The housing association or co-operative will usually have had the rent registered.

Once a rent has been registered, a new rent cannot usually be considered for the accommodation for two years. The rent can only be increased if:-

- you ask for a new fair rent assessment after two years
- your landlord asks for a new fair rent assessment after one year and nine months, although any new rent would not become effective until the end of two years.

An application for a rent increase can be made earlier, but only if the tenancy has changed drastically or if you and your landlord apply together. If you need help paying the rent you may be able to claim housing benefit.

Assured tenants
Housing association or housing co-operative tenancies which began on or after 15 January 1989

Many housing association tenants whose tenancy started on or after 15 January 1989 are assured tenants. If you are an assured tenant, your rent is the rent you agreed to pay your landlord at the beginning of the tenancy and should be covered in your tenancy agreement. The tenancy agreement should also state when and how the rent can be increased.

In England, most housing associations and housing co-operatives are registered with the Homes and Communities Agency and must follow standards and procedures set down by this regulatory body. They are sometimes known as social landlords. They set rents in accordance with government guidance and tenants have to be given clear information about how their rent and service charges are set and how they can be changed.

You may have the right to apply to a Rent Assessment Committee if you do not agree to a rent increase.

In Wales, housing associations must manage their housing to standards set by the Welsh Government. You must be informed in writing, and in advance about any changes in your rent. You should be given at least 28 days notice of any increase. You may have the right to apply to a Rent Assessment Committee if you do not agree to a rent increase.

If you are a housing association tenant in Wales, there is a leaflet explaining your rights called The Guarantee for Housing Association Residents. You can find this on the Welsh Government website at: www.new.wales.gov.uk.

If you want to apply to a Rent Assessment Committee you should consult an experienced adviser, for example, a Citizens Advice Bureau. If you need help paying the rent you may be able to claim housing benefit.

You may also be entitled to other benefits if you are on a low income or you are unemployed.

To work out which other benefits you may be entitled to, you should consult an experienced adviser, for example, a Citizens Advice Bureau.

Affordable rent

Affordable rent is a type of social housing provided in England by social housing landlords.

The rent is called 'affordable' but it is a higher rent than would normally be charged for social housing. The landlord can charge up to 80% of what it would cost if you were renting the property privately. The extra money from affordable rent homes goes towards building more new social housing.

In most cases, tenancies on affordable rent terms are granted by housing associations. Where the landlord is a housing association, the type of tenancy granted is either an assured or an assured shorthold tenancy. In some cases, a local authority may grant a tenancy on affordable rent terms. Where it does, the tenancy type is either a secure or a flexible tenancy.

An affordable rent can be increased once a year. The maximum amount that an affordable rent can be increased by is Retail Price Index (RPI) + 0.5 %.

If you are on benefits or have a low income you may qualify for housing benefit to help pay some or all of the affordable rent.

Repairs and improvements

As a tenant you have the right to have your accommodation kept in a reasonable state of repair. You have also an obligation to look after the accommodation. The tenancy agreement may give more details of both your landlord's and your responsibilities in carrying out repairs and you should check this. We have discussed repairs earlier in the book.

Certain repairs will almost always be your landlord's responsibility, whether or not they are specifically mentioned in the tenancy agreement. These are:-

- the structure and exterior of the premises (such as walls, floors and window frames), and the drains, gutters and external pipes. If the property is a house, the essential means of access to it, such as steps from the street, are also included in 'structure and exterior'. It also includes garden paths and steps
- the water and gas pipes and electrical wiring (including, for example, taps and sockets)
- the basins, sinks, baths and toilets
- fixed heaters (for example, gas fires) and water heaters but not gas or electric cookers.

The Right to repair

Tenants of local authorities and other social landlords (including housing associations) can use 'right to repair' schemes to claim compensation for repairs which the landlord does not carry out within a set timescale.

Local authority tenants have a right to repair scheme which they must follow. Under the scheme, if repairs are not carried out within a fixed time scale, you can notify your landlord that you want a different contractor to do the job. The local authority must appoint a new contractor and set another time limit. You can then claim compensation if the repair is not carried out within the new time limit.

As a local authority tenant, you can currently use the 'right to repair' scheme for repairs which your landlord estimates would cost up to £250. You can also claim up to £50 compensation. Twenty types of repairs qualify for the scheme, including insecure doors, broken entry phone systems, blocked sinks and leaking roofs.

A repair will not qualify for the scheme if the local authority has fewer than 100 properties, is not responsible for the repair or if the authority decides it would cost more than £250.

If you're the tenant of another social landlord, such as a housing association, you are entitled to compensation if you report a repair or maintenance problem which affects your health, safety or security and your landlord fails twice to make the repair within the set timescale.

There is a flat rate award which is currently £10, plus £2 a day up to a total of £50, for each day the repair remains outstanding. A maximum cost for an eligible repair may be set by the individual landlord.

Improvements

As a local authority tenant if you make certain improvements to your home, for example, loft insulation, draught proofing, new baths, basins and toilets and security measures, you can apply for compensation for doing so when you move out. You will not be eligible for this compensation if you buy your home.

Disabled tenants

If you are disabled, you may be able to have alterations carried out to your home. You may first have to get the need for any alterations assessed by the social services department. Alterations could include the installation of a stair lift or hoist or adaptation of a bathroom or toilet.

If you want to get an alteration carried out you should consult an experienced adviser, for example, at a Citizens Advice Bureau.

A disabled tenant may also be able to get a disabled facilities grant to make the home more suitable.

Gas appliances

Your landlord must make sure that any gas appliances in residential premises are safe. They must arrange for safety checks on appliances and fittings to be carried out at least once every twelve months. The inspection must be carried out by someone who is registered with Gas Safety Register. Their website is: www.gassaferegister.co.uk. The landlord must also keep a record of the date of the check, any problems identified and any action taken. As the tenant, you have the right to see this record as long as you give reasonable notice.

If your landlord does not arrange for checks or refuses to allow you to see the record of the check, you could contact the local Health and Safety Executive office.

The right to stay in the accommodation

This is an outline of the rights you have as a tenant of a local authority, housing association or housing co-operative to stay in your accommodation and how you can be evicted.

Secure tenants

As a secure tenant you have the right to stay in the accommodation as long as you keep to the terms of the tenancy agreement with your landlord. However, if the tenancy agreement is broken, for example, because of rent arrears or nuisance to neighbours, your landlord can serve a notice on you and apply to the county court for eviction.

A social housing landlord can only evict you if they give you the proper notice and if one of the 'grounds for possession' applies.

What constitutes 'grounds for possession' is complicated and someone whose landlord is seeking eviction should consult an experienced adviser, for example, at a Citizens Advice Bureau.

. The landlord must apply to the county court to seek possession of the property and a secure tenant can only be evicted if the court grants a possession order to the landlord.

Assured tenants

As an assured tenant you have the right to stay in the accommodation as long as you keep to the terms of the tenancy agreement with your landlord. However, if the tenancy agreement is broken, for example, because of rent arrears or nuisance to neighbours, your landlord can serve a notice on you.

The housing association will then have to obtain a possession order from the county court by proving that one of the 'grounds for possession' applies. We discussed grounds for possession earlier in the book.

Social housing tenancies and discrimination

When renting accommodation from a local authority, housing association or other social landlord, they must not discriminate against you because of your disability, gender reassignment, pregnancy and maternity, race, religion or belief, sex or sexual orientation. This means that they are not allowed to:

- rent a property to you on worse terms than other tenants
- treat you differently from other tenants in the way you are allowed to use facilities such as a laundry or a garden
- evict or harass you because of discrimination
- charge you higher rent than other tenants
- refuse to re-house you because of discrimination
- refuse to carry out repairs to your home because of disrimination
- refuse to make reasonable changes to a property or a term in the tenancy agreement which would allow a disabled person to live there.

If you think your landlord is discriminating against you, you should get advice from an experienced adviser, for example, at a Citizens Advice Bureau.

Introductory tenants

Some local authorities make all new tenants introductory tenants for the first 12 months of the tenancy.

Rights of introductory tenants

Introductory tenants have some but not all of the rights of secure tenants. The table overleaf shows your rights as an introductory tenant compared with secure tenants.

Statutory right	Secure tenant	Introductory tenant
Right to succession by partners or in some cases family members	yes	yes
Right to repair	yes	yes
Right to assign	yes	no
Right to buy	yes	no, but period spent as an introductory tenant counts towards the discount
Right to take in lodgers	yes	no
Right to sub-let part of your home	yes	no
Right to do improvements	yes	no
Right to exchange your home with certain other tenants	yes	no
Right to vote prior to transfer to new landlord	yes	no
Right to be consulted on housing management issues	yes	yes
Right to be consulted on decision to delegate housing management	yes	yes
Right to participate in housing management contract monitoring	yes	yes

Ending an introductory tenancy

At the end of the twelve months, provided there have been no possession proceedings against you, the introductory tenancy will usually be converted by your landlord to a secure tenancy. However, your landlord may decide to extend the introductory tenancy for a further six months. If this happens, you will be told the reasons for the decision and given the chance to ask for the decision to be reviewed.

Possession proceedings

It is very easy for a landlord to evict an introductory tenant. If you have received a notice from the landlord stating that they intend to evict you and take possession of the property, you should immediately consult an experienced adviser, for example, at a Citizens Advice Bureau.

Flexible tenants

Flexible tenancies are a type of tenancy that can be granted by local authority landlords in England, from 1 April 2012. Not all local authorities offer them.

A flexible tenancy is similar to a local authority secure tenancy. However, a secure tenancy is periodic, which means that it lasts for an indefinite period of time. Periodic tenancies are often called 'lifetime tenancies'. In contrast, a flexible tenancy lasts for a fixed period of time. In most cases, a flexible tenancy will last for at least five years.

A local authority has to serve a written notice on you before a flexible tenancy can start. The notice must tell you that the tenancy you're being offered is a flexible tenancy, and what the terms of the tenancy are.

Flexible tenants have a number of legal rights, many of which are similar to the rights of secure tenants. For example, the right to pass on your tenancy when you're alive or when you die, the right to exchange your home with certain other tenants, and the right to buy your home.

A local authority doesn't have to grant you another tenancy when the fixed term of the flexible tenancy comes to an end. You can ask the local authority to review its decision not to grant you another tenancy. The review will consider if your landlord has followed its policies and procedures when making that decision.

If you are not given another tenancy when your flexible tenancy comes to an end, the local authority will take action to evict you.

Right-to-buy.

Perhaps the most valuable right enjoyed by a secure tenant is the right to buy either the freehold, in the case of a house, or the leasehold, in the case of a flat. In order to claim this right there is also a residence qualification to fulfill. The tenant, or the tenants spouse must have been resident as a secure tenant (not necessarily in the same property) for five years prior to the application to buy. Currently, the government is in the process of extending the right to buy to Housing Association tenants and reducing the residence requirements.

Discounts

If you qualify for Right to Buy, you can get a discount on the market value of your home when you buy it.

The maximum discount is £77,900 (2017) across England, except in London boroughs where it's £103,900. The discount is based on:

- how long you've been a tenant with a public sector landlord
- the type of property you're buying (a flat or a house)
- the value of your home

If you're buying with someone else, you count the years of whoever's been a public sector tenant the longest.

You'll usually have to repay some or all your discount if you sell your home within 5 years.

The discount you get might be reduced if you've used Right to Buy in the past.

Working out the discount

There are different discount levels for houses and flats.

For houses you get a 35% discount if you've been a public sector tenant for between 3 and 5 years. For every extra year you've been a public sector tenant, the discount goes up by 1%, up to a maximum of 70% – or £77,900 across England and £103,900 in London boroughs (whichever is lower).

For flats you get a 50% discount if you've been a public sector tenant for between 3 and 5 years. For every extra year you've been a public sector tenant, the discount goes up by 2%, up to a maximum of 70% – or £79,900 across England and £103,900 in London boroughs (whichever is lower).

If your landlord has spent money on your home

Your discount will be less if your landlord has spent money building or maintaining your home:

- in the last 10 years - if your landlord built or acquired your home before 2 April 2012
- in the last 15 years - if you are buying your home through Preserved Right to Buy, or if your landlord acquired your home after 2 April 2012

If your landlord has spent more money than your home is now worth, you won't get any discount.

Social HomeBuy

If you can't afford to buy your home through Right to Buy, you may still be able to buy a share of it through social homebuy. With Social HomeBuy, you buy a share of your council or housing association home and pay rent on the rest of it.

Discounts

You'll get a discount of between £9,000 and £16,000 on the value of your home, depending on:
- where your home is
- the size of the share you're buying

If you want to buy another share in your home later on, you'll get a discount on that too.

Buying more of your home later

You must buy at least 25% of your home. You can buy more later, until you own 100%. This is called 'staircasing'.

If you buy more of your home, your rent will go down - because it's based on how much of the property you rent. Your landlord can charge rent of up to 3% of the value of their share of your home, per year.

Example

Your home is worth £240,000 and you buy a 50% share. Your landlord charges you 3% rent on their 50% share. 3% of £120,000 is £3,600 per year. This works out at £300 per month for you to pay in rent.

Who can't apply

You can't use Social HomeBuy if:

- you have an assured shorthold tenancy
- you're being made bankrupt
- a court has ordered you to leave your home
- your landlord is taking action against you for rent arrears, anti-social behaviour or for breaking your tenancy agreement

Not all local councils or housing associations have joined the scheme. Check with your landlord to find out if they belong to the scheme and whether your home is included.

Right to acquire

Right to Acquire allows most housing association tenants to buy their home at a discount. You apply using the Right to Acquire application form.

You can apply to buy your housing association home if you've had a public sector landlord for 3 years. These landlords include:

- housing associations
- councils
- the armed services
- NHS trusts and foundation trusts

Eligible properties

Your property must either have been:

- built or bought by a housing association after 31 March 1997 (and funded through a social housing grant provided by the Housing Corporation or local council)
- transferred from a local council to a housing association after 31 March 1997
- Your landlord must be registered with the Homes and Communities Agency.

The home you want to buy must also be:

- a self-contained property
- your only or main home

Who doesn't qualify

You can't use Right to Acquire if:

- you're being made bankrupt
- a court has ordered you to leave your home
- you're a council tenant – you may be able to use Right to Buy instead
- you have 'Preserved Right to Buy'

Discounts

You can get a discount of between £9,000 and £16,000 on the price of your property. The amount of discount you'll get depends on where you live in the

Succession and assured and secure tenancies

For secure tenancies, it can be found under Section 160 of the Localism Act 2011; while for assured tenancies, it is under Section 161 of the same Act.

It remains that there can only be one succession, and that when one joint tenant dies this counts as one succession.

Before the Localism Act, a wide range of family members were able to succeed to a tenancy on the death of a secure tenant, including: civil partners, parents, grandparents, children, grandchildren, aunts, uncles, nieces, nephews, and adopted children. A full list is set out at Section 113 of the Housing Act 1985.

Civil partners and spouses are entitled to succeed so long as they were occupying the property as their only or principal home at the date of the death.

Other family members were required to prove they had occupied the property as their only or principal home for 12 months prior to the death of the tenant whose tenancy they wish to succeed.

Under the provisions of Section 17 Housing Act 1988, a spouse, civil partner or someone living with the tenant as a spouse or civil partner is entitled to succeed to the tenancy provided they occupied the property as their only or principal home at the date of death.

It was very common to see landlords of assured tenants including wider succession rights in their tenancy agreements, thus allowing the tenant to benefit from a wider list of family members who would be entitled to succeed to the tenancy provided they had occupied the property as their only or principal home as the death of the tenant.

Automatic right to succession

Section 160 of the Localism Act 2011 provides that secure tenancies which started after 1 April 2012 are limited to the succession of spouses or civil partners. This is an automatic right.

The wider group of family members who have traditionally succeeded to a secure tenancy by virtue of being listed in Section 113 of the Housing Act 1985 do not automatically receive statutory succession. The landlord can make express provision in the tenancy agreement to expand the group of individuals that can succeed.

Section 161 of the Localism Act 2011 provides that assured tenancies which started after 1 April 2012 containing a clause which expands the statutory group of individuals entitled to succeed to include family members; the family member who is entitled to succeed will enjoy a statutory succession. Family members may only succeed if there is express provision in the tenancy agreement.

Unlike before, those listed and who become entitled to succeed under an express term of a tenancy agreement will enjoy a statutory succession, so that no new tenancy is required.

****

OWNER OCCUPIERS AND THE LAW

12

THE LAW AND OWNER OCCUPIERS-
COMMONHOLD, FREEHOLD AND
LEASEHOLD

Commonhold and Leasehold Reform Act 2002

The Commonhold and Leasehold Reform Act 2002 introduced into English law an entirely new form of tenure, namely commonhold. It is specifically targeted at blocks of flats, where leasehold has been the normal form of tenure until now. We will discuss commonhold briefly a little later, suffice to say that with such an arrangement in a block of flats the commonholders own all the common parts together with leases being abolished.

Freehold and Leasehold

The law does not look at property in the same way as most lay people. Most people think in terms of houses and other buildings; the law is more interested in the land beneath. A freehold home owner will say "I own my house." But the law will say "He owns the land on which is built the house he lives in." To the law, the key point is that he owns the land - the buildings on it are incidental.

For practical purposes, the strongest form of title to land is that of freehold. Freehold title lasts forever; it may be bought and sold, or passed by inheritance. In short, freehold title is tantamount to outright ownership, and is taken as such for the purposes of this book.

Freeholders may, of course, use their land for their own purposes. The freehold home owner is merely the most familiar example. But they may also, if they wish, allow other people to use their land. And this is where leases, and other forms of tenure, come in.

Suppose you would like to make use of a piece of land owned by someone else. The owner is unwilling to sell it to you, but, having no immediate use for it himself, is willing to allow you to use it for a time, perhaps in exchange for payment. At its simplest, this arrangement implies no more than a licence - the owner's (i.e. landlord's) permission for you to be on his land.

But such a licence can be revoked by the landlord at any time, with or without a good reason. As such it is not very valuable, so if the owner wants to make money by allowing other people to use his land, he needs to give them a legal status that they will be willing to pay for. This is achieved by granting a lease or tenancy. It should be noted here that, from the legal point of view, a lease and a tenancy are the same thing; but in practice, the terms tend to be used in different contexts. This is explained below: for the present, we shall call it a lease.

A lease grants the leaseholder permission to use the land for a certain period, which can be anything from a day or two to several thousand years. It will usually attach conditions, for example that the leaseholder must pay rent (usually a sum of money, although in principle other goods or services could constitute rent).

The lease may, but does not have to, put certain restrictions on what the leaseholder may do with the land. But it must, in order to be a lease rather than merely a licence, grant the leaseholder 'exclusive possession'. This is the right to exclude other people, especially the landlord, from the land. Such a right need not be absolute, and exceptions to it are explained later in the book: but it is enough to give the leaseholder a high degree of control over the land, which has become, for the duration of the lease, very much the leaseholder's land rather than the freeholder's. A lease, unless it contains a stipulation to the contrary, may be bought, sold, or inherited; if this happens, all the rights and duties under it pass to the new owner.

Leases and Tenancies
Confusion is often caused by the fact that, although the terms leaseholder

(or lessee) and tenant are legally interchangeable, they tend to be used in different senses. The tendency is to refer to short leases as tenancies: the more substantial the rights conferred, and the longer the period for which they run, the likelier it is that the agreement will be referred to as a lease. For the purposes of this book, an agreement will be referred to as a 'tenancy' if it is periodic or runs for a fixed term of less than seven years. A fixed term agreement running for more than seven years will be referred to as a 'lease'.

A 'periodic' tenancy is one that runs from period to period (usually, from week to week or month to month) until something intervenes to stop it, and is conditional on payment of rent. A tenancy that runs for a fixed term of less than seven years has a definite date of expiry but is otherwise similar to a periodic tenancy and will depend on regular payment of rent. Tenancies granted by local authorities and housing associations tend to be periodic; private landlords generally grant either periodic tenancies or short fixed-term tenancies (typically, six months). At any rate, the landlord of a periodic or short-term tenancy will usually accept most of the responsibility for maintaining the property and will charge a relatively high rent to allow for this. If the tenancy is for residential property, the landlord's duty to maintain the dwelling is imposed by law (Landlord and Tenant Act 1985).

It is common for private landlords to insist on prepayment of rent or a deposit before granting a tenancy, and many landlords will levy a separate service charge to cover the cost of some activities that are peripheral to the central one of providing housing; but despite these costs it would be true to say that the principal financial responsibility accepted by a periodic or short-term tenant is that of paying the rent.

The position of a leaseholder is very different. The major financial commitment will usually be a substantial initial payment either to the landlord (if the lease is newly created) or to the previous leaseholder. There is still a rent, called a ground rent, payable to the landlord, but it is usually a notional amount (£50 or £100 a year is not uncommon). Its purpose is not so much to give the landlord an income as to give the leaseholder an annual reminder that ultimate ownership of the land is not his.

Types of Leasehold Property

In the context of residential property, it should be noted that the great majority of leases relate to flats rather than houses. This is because of the legal concept of land tenure as described above. If a builder buys some freehold land and covers it in houses, it is possible to parcel out the area so that each bit of freehold land, and the house standing on it, can be sold separately. It does not matter if the houses are semi-detached or terraced, because there is well-established law governing party walls of adjoining freeholders. But if there are flats, the builder has a problem: how can the flats be sold since they cannot be said to stand on separate and distinct bits of land? The answer is to sell leases.

Where flats are sold, each purchaser acquires a lease that gives him specified rights over the parcel of land on which the flats stand. These rights, of course, are shared by the leaseholders of the other flats. In addition, however, each leaseholder gains the right to exclusive possession of part of the building occupying the land - his own flat. The leaseholder would say "I own my flat", but the law says "He owns a lease granting him certain rights, in particular that of access, to a defined parcel of land and the right of exclusive possession of specified parts of a building erected on that land." This may seem a slightly unusual way of looking at it, but it is fundamental to understanding the way that the law sees the relationship between leaseholders of flats and their freeholders.

The freehold of flatted property will often be retained by the developer, although sometimes it will be sold to a property company. Formerly, it was common practice for the freehold to be retained even when separate houses were built. This allowed the freeholder to retain an interest in the property and, above all, to regain full possession of it when the lease expired. However, the position of freeholders has been weakened by three key pieces of legislation, the Leasehold Reform Act 1967, the Leasehold Reform, Housing and Urban Development Act 1993, and the Commonhold and Leasehold Reform Act 2002. These Acts are described in detail further on: their overall effect is to entitle leaseholders either to the freehold of houses or to a new lease of flats. In view of the legislation, there is now little point in the original owner's attempting to retain the freehold of land on which houses have been built. The exception is where a house is sold on the basis of shared ownership - see below.

Most residential leasehold property therefore consists of flats. Of these, most are in the private sector, comprising purpose-built blocks and (especially in London) conversions of what were once large single houses. The freehold will usually belong to the developer, to a property company, or sometimes to the original owner of the site.

House leases normally give most of the repairing responsibility to the leaseholder - services provided by the freeholder, and therefore service charges, are minimal. In flats, however, although the leaseholder will normally be responsible for the interior of the flat, the freeholder will maintain the fabric of the building and will recoup the costs of doing so by levying service charges on the leaseholders. This is an area of such potential conflict between leaseholders and freeholders that it has been the subject of legislation. It is dealt with fully further on in the book.

Mixed-tenure blocks: the right to buy

The general shift from renting to owning means that sometimes flats have been sold in blocks that were originally developed for letting to tenants: the result is often a 'mixed-tenure' block, with both leaseholders and tenants. Although this sometimes happens in the private sector, it is particularly common in blocks owned by local authorities and housing associations, for it is to these that the statutory right to buy applies. This right was created by the Housing Act 1980 and allows most local authority tenants, and some housing association tenants, to buy their homes at a heavily discounted price. Tenants of houses are normally sold the freehold, but tenants of flats become leaseholders.

Shared ownership

Another result of the trend towards home ownership has been the dramatic expansion of shared ownership. This is a form of tenure that combines leasing and renting. However, the term 'shared ownership' is something of a misnomer because ownership is not, in fact, shared between the leaseholder and the freeholder. The lease relates to the whole property, not part of it, and the shared owner is as entitled as any other leaseholder to consider himself the owner of his house. The key point about shared ownership leases is not that they give an inferior form of tenure to other leases but that they have different conditions attached. The leaseholder pays less than the full value of the lease; typically, half. In exchange for this concession, he pays not the normal notional ground rent but a much more substantial rent. However, he is much more a leaseholder than he is a tenant, and, like other leaseholders (but unlike tenants) is responsible for the internal repair of the property and, in the case of houses, usually the fabric of the building too.

Shared owners usually have the right to increase their stake as and when they can afford it: this is called 'staircasing' because the owner's share goes up in steps. If the property is a house, the freehold will normally be transferred when the owner's share reaches 100%, and he will then be in the same position as any other freehold home owner. If it is a flat, he will continue to be a leaseholder but there will no longer be a rental (other than ground rent).

Head Leases and Subleases

For the sake of clarity and brevity, this book has been written throughout on the basis that there are only two parties involved: the freeholder and the leaseholder. Usually this picture is accurate; but it is the right of the leaseholder, unless the lease specifically forbids it, to sublet the property, or part of it, to someone else. This means that the leaseholder delegates some of his rights over the property to another person. Obviously, he cannot delegate rights greater than his own, so that if he holds a lease of the property running until 2025 he cannot grant a sublease running until 2050. And he cannot grant a sublease of the whole of his rights because this would leave him with no interest in the property: it would, in fact, amount to the same as an assignment. So it is necessary for a sublease that the original leaseholder be left with something; either some period of time or some part of the property.

It is possible in theory to have a whole hierarchy of leases applying to a particular property, starting with the freehold, then the head lease, then a sublease, followed by sub-subleases and possibly sub-sub-subleases below those. There are two rules that limit this kind of proliferation: one, explained above, is that each lease must confer less, in space or time or both, than the one above it; and the other, that is a lease may not be held by the same person as holds the lease (or freehold) immediately above it.

Commonhold

To try to deal with problems arising from the relationship between freeholders and leaseholders, a new form of tenure, 'commonhold', was created by the Commonhold and Leasehold Reform Act 2002. It is designed specifically for use in blocks of flats, and the idea is that all the individual flat owners (or 'unit holders', as the Act calls them) will belong to a 'commonhold association', a registered company that operate under a constitution (the 'memorandum and articles') and act in accordance with a 'commonhold community statement'. This arrangement ensures that each unit holder will have two separate interests in relation to the property: individually, and collectively, in the block as a whole.

****

13

OBLIGATIONS OF FREEHOLDER AND LEASEHOLDER

General Principles

For centuries the law did little to regulate the relationship between freeholders and leaseholders. The view was taken that they had entered into the relationship of their own free will, and it was up to them to agree whatever terms and conditions they liked. If either party did not keep the bargain, he could of course be sued in the courts, but, on the whole, the law did not interfere in the bargain itself.

In the twentieth century, however, the view grew up that some types of bargain are inherently unfair and even those that are not might still be open to exploitation.

An example of the first type is an agreement that residential property will revert to the original freeholder at the end of a long lease. This meant that when 99-year leases expired, leaseholders found that their homes had abruptly returned to the outright ownership of the heir of the original freeholder, leaving them as mere trespassers liable to be ejected at any time. In practice, freeholders were usually willing to grant a fresh lease, but sometimes only at a very high price that the leaseholder might well be unable to afford. In some cases, freeholders insisted on reclaiming the property however much the leaseholder offered, and the law supported them. This is the state of affairs that led to legislation entitling almost all residential leaseholders to extend their leases, and many of them to claim the freehold.

The freeholder's right to demand a service charge is an example of an arrangement that is fair in principle but open to abuse in practice. It is inevitable, especially in flats, that responsibility for some types of repair cannot be ascribed to any individual leaseholder and must therefore be retained by the freeholder; who must, in turn, recoup the cost from leaseholders. However, some freeholders abused this system by levying extravagant service charges that made the service charge a source of profit. To prevent this, there is now a substantial body of legislation designed to ensure that freeholders carry out only the works that are really necessary and that they recover their legitimate costs and no more. The complicated rules governing this are chiefly found in the Landlord and Tenant Act 1985 (as amended) and are described in Chapter Three.

Under the Landlord and Tenant Act 1987, either party to a long lease (one originally granted for at least 21 years) may go to the First Tier Tribunal to argue that the lease is deficient in some way and needs to be changed. If only the one lease is affected, the tribunal may vary it. Sometimes, however, a number of leases may need to be changed; in this case either the freeholder or 75% of the leaseholders may apply.

Obligations of Leaseholders

The obligations of leaseholders are set out in the lease; indeed, since it is a document drafted by or on behalf of freeholders, one of its main aims is to tell leaseholders what they must and must not do. However, legislation and judicial decisions sometimes come to the leaseholder's assistance.

Consumer legislation can also apply to leases; in particular, the Unfair Terms in Consumer Contracts Regulations 1999 (which replace earlier regulations made in 1995) have a major impact. These apply to standard terms in contracts. This means they normally cover the terms of leases, which are usually presented to potential leaseholders as a package with no opportunity to renegotiate individual terms.

Occasionally, however, individual terms can be specifically negotiated and it should be noted that in that case the Unfair Terms Regulations do not apply. Nor will they apply to any lease granted before the earlier version of the regulations which came in July 1995. The Office of Fair Trading has issued advice about the types of term that are likely to be judged unfair in the context of assured tenancies. The OFT has not issued advice about long leases, but it is likely that similar standards would apply.

a: *Plain and intelligible language*

Over many years property lawyers have developed an obscure and technical language that can have the effect of excluding outsiders. This form of 'legalese' is characterised by unwieldy sentences with few (or no) commas to break them up, long lists often consisting of different names for the same thing, and a vocabulary of unfamiliar words and (worst of all) familiar words given unfamiliar meanings.

For instance, in normal English the verb 'determine' means 'ascertain' or 'firmly decide', but when a property lawyer applies it to a lease it means 'end' or 'terminate' (as in 'the lease shall determine if…'). Property lawyers also have a well-merited reputation for using words like 'hereinafter' and 'aforesaid', which, although not ambiguous, are hardly everyday English, while occasional outbreaks of Latin are not unknown (*pari passu* and *mutatis mutandis*).

Thankfully, this style is going out of fashion and an increasing number of modern leases are being written in more intelligible language, and for leases made since 1995 the Unfair Terms Regulations mean that arcanely written terms may be unenforceable. However, a huge number of leases written in traditional style still have decades or even centuries to run, so unfortunately property lawyers' English will be with us for a long time yet.

b: Terms Unfair on Consumers

There are some terms to which the Office of Fair Trading objects in any consumer contract. These are terms that place an unreasonable burden on the customer (the leaseholder) or give an unfair advantage to the supplier (the freeholder). Some of these terms are common in long leases.

There may be a clause in which the leaseholder declares that he has 'read and understood' the lease, even though the document is long and complex and it unlikely that anyone would read (or understand) the whole of it. The aim is to put the leaseholder at a disadvantage in any dispute by arguing that he was fully aware of all the terms of the lease. Another way of loading the scales is a clause allowing the freeholder the final decision about vital matters, such as whether or not the freeholder and the leaseholder have fulfilled their respective obligations under the lease.

These clauses are probably unenforceable in leases made since July 1995, but in earlier leases they are probably valid.

There are other types of clause that are potentially a problem for the leaseholder. An example is a clause laying down procedural formalities. Such a clause is not necessarily a problem: for instance, leases commonly require formal communications between the freeholder and the leaseholder to be in writing, and this is a perfectly reasonable requirement because it reduces the chances misunderstandings or disputes about who said what. But it is harder to justify a requirement for notices to be sent by registered post, and some leases stipulate procedures that are so onerous that the aim seems to be to deter leaseholders from exercising their rights.

Similar comments apply to clauses imposing financial penalties for breaches of the lease. This is not necessarily unreasonable, but sometimes the penalties are out of all proportion to the nature of the breach.

Some leases require the leaseholder to join with the freeholder (and help with the cost) in responding to legal or other notices pertaining to the property. Again, this may be reasonable in some circumstances, but as a blanket requirement it can act against leaseholders' interests.

An interesting and debatable issue is the prohibition of set-off, which is a standard clause in most leases. 'Set-off' is the practice of deducting (or 'setting off') from any payment made by one party under an agreement any sums that are owed by the other party. For instance, suppose a leaseholder considers that a repair to the fabric of the building is the freeholder's responsibility, but the freeholder either disputes this or fails to take any action. Eventually the leaseholder does the work at his own expense, and next time the annual service charge falls due he reimburses himself by deducting, or 'setting off', the cost from his service charge payment.

Leaseholders like set-off because it is an easy way of reclaiming disputed sums from the freeholder, and it shifts onto the freeholder the onus of continuing the dispute. Freeholders dislike it for exactly the same reasons, which is why leases normally prohibit it. The Office of Fair Trading, in its advice on assured tenancies, says that prohibiting set-off is unfair, but it is not clear whether the same advice would apply to leases.

The possibility that unfair, or potentially unfair, clauses will feature in a lease underlines the need for competent legal advice before signing it. An experienced solicitor will be able to advise whether doubtful clauses can be, or are likely to be, used against leaseholders. Leaseholders may also have remedies available under the Landlord and Tenant Act: this is covered below and, in the key area of service charges, in the next Chapter.

c: Restrictive clauses in leases

So far, we have looked at leases as if they were consumer contracts, and outlined some of the clauses they may contain that could affect leaseholders in their capacity as consumers. But there are some further potentially difficult terms that relate specifically to property issues. These terms are not necessarily unreasonable. For example, in a lease concerning an upstairs flat it would be quite normal to have a clause requiring the leaseholder to keep the premises carpeted. This makes sense because bare floors, although currently very fashionable, could be very noisy for the people in the flat below.

The Office of Fair Trading's advice identifies several types of sweeping provisions that would, if they were enforced, considerably restrict the tenant's ability to live a normal life. Although the OFT's advice relates to assured tenancies, similar objections would probably apply to these clauses in leases. For example:

- Pets Leases often lay down that the leaseholder may not own pets, or may not do so without the freeholder's permission.
- Upkeep Leases may say that the leaseholder must decorate periodically - say, every five or seven years. Where there is a garden, it is common for the leaseholder to be required to keep it in good order.

- Business Leases often lay down that the leaseholder must not run any sort of business from his home.

- Use as residence A lease will generally say that the property is to be used for the residential purposes of the leaseholder and his household, and that it cannot be sublet. It will sometimes attempt to restrict how many people may live there apart from the leaseholder.

- Other Leases sometimes forbid such things as the keeping of flammable materials and the installation of television aerials or satellite dishes. They may require leaseholders to drain hot water systems whenever they are away, or keep the premises clean and free of dust.

It is easy to see why freeholders want such clauses in the lease: it is because they realise that there will be serious problems if someone attempts, for instance, to keep four alsatians in a studio flat. The neighbours will be inconvenienced and will complain to the freeholder, and leases of other flats in the same block will become difficult to sell.

The same arguments could apply if one of the leaseholders allows his flat to fall into complete decorative decay or if he runs a noisy and busy trade from his home.

But the kind of blanket rules that appear in many leases go too far. A rule against any pets at all forbids not only four noisy alsatians but also entirely inoffensive pets such as a budgie or a goldfish. In the same way, prohibiting business activities means that the leaseholder may not use his home to write a book for publication, or address envelopes, and so on - types of home working that could not possibly inconvenience anyone.

The rule against sub-letting also prevents leaseholders from exploiting the value of their property by letting it out, something that is open to most home-owners and is increasingly accepted as normal.

For leases made since July 1995, these sweeping clauses are probably unfair and unenforceable. But even for older leases, the reality is that such broad provisions are seldom enforced. Freeholders, and their lawyers, like them because they feel that they preserve their freedom of action, allowing them to decide whether or not to enforce the lease if it is clear that one of these blanket conditions is being broken. But there are two problems with this attitude.

The first is that it creates uncertainty in the minds of leaseholders. Suppose the leases in a block of flats prohibit all pets, but leaseholder A has a goldfish and no action has been taken even though the freeholder is aware of the infringement. Leaseholder B may well conclude that there will be no objection if he gets a cat. If still there is no action, leaseholder C may feel able to get a couple of dogs - and so on. So the fact that restrictions are so broad can have the paradoxical effect of reducing their effectiveness.

The second problem is that if, in the example just given, the freeholder takes legal action to force C to get rid of the dogs, it is possible that C will argue in court that the treatment of the other leaseholders shows that the freeholder is not seriously interested in banning pets and that the action has been motivated rather by petty spite or bias.

It would be better if freeholders and their lawyers drafted leases that say what they mean: not that leaseholders may have no pets at all, but that they may have no pets apt to damage the property or cause inconvenience or annoyance to other persons. The same principle should apply to clauses dealing with sub-letting or working from home.

It is unfortunate that this book is forced to advise leaseholders to ignore some parts of their leases. The responsibility for this, however, lies with freeholders and their lawyers for writing into standard leases blanket conditions purporting to prohibit entirely inoffensive behaviour. This practice makes it inevitable, in the real world that leaseholders will disregard certain clauses, and that books like this will have to give them some indication of when they can probably do so safely. Most leaseholders exercise common sense and realise that the freeholder is unlikely to take action unless there is a complaint, which means that the leaseholder may do almost whatever he pleases provided he refrains from provoking anyone. It is sensible to stay on good terms with neighbours to ensure that if anything is bothering them they take it up directly with you rather than report the matter to the freeholder. Other leaseholders will also be able to tell you what view has been taken in the past - both by other residents and by the freeholder - in doubtful cases.

d: Restrictions on sale

Some leases restrict the kind of person to whom the lease may be sold (or 'assigned' - see below). For example, a housing scheme may have been intended specifically for the elderly. Clearly, it will not be maintained as such if leaseholders are free to assign or bequeath their leases to whomever they please, so the lease will say that it may be assigned only to persons above a certain age, and that if it is inherited by anyone outside the age group it must be sold on to someone qualified to hold it. Although this could be described as an onerous term because it makes it more difficult to find a buyer and may reduce the lease's value, it is reasonable given the need to ensure that the scheme continues to house elderly people exclusively. And the restriction it imposes is not too severe because so many potential purchasers qualify.

However, some leases define much more narrowly to whom they may be sold. Sometimes the freeholder is a body owned and run by the leaseholders themselves, and in these cases it is usual to require that all leaseholders must join the organisation and, if they leave it, must immediately dispose of the lease to someone that is willing to join. Again, such a term is not necessarily unacceptable. If the organisation makes relatively light demands on its members (perhaps no more than a modest admission fee or annual subscription), the restriction is unlikely greatly to diminish the value of the lease. If, however, the organisation expects much more from its members - perhaps that they actively take part in running it, or that they pay a large annual subscription - the value of the lease will be severely reduced because it will be difficult to find purchasers willing to accept the conditions. A key point is whether the organisation has power to expel members, thus forcing them to sell; and, if so, in what circumstances and by whom this power can be exercised.

e: Access

Virtually any lease will contain a clause allowing the freeholder to enter the property in order to inspect or repair it. This has the effect of qualifying the leaseholder's right of exclusive possession (see below), but only subject to certain conditions. The freeholder (or the freeholder's servants, such as agents or contractors) may enter only at reasonable times, and subject to the giving of reasonable notice. If these conditions are not met, the leaseholder is under no obligation to allow them in; and, even when the conditions are met, the landlord will be trespassing if he enters the property without the leaseholder's consent. If the leaseholder refuses consent even though the time is reasonable and reasonable notice has been given, the landlord's remedy is to get a court order against the leaseholder compelling him to grant entry. It is probable, in such a case, that the landlord will seek, and get, an award of legal costs against the leaseholder.

f: Arbitration
Many leases contain clauses providing that disputes can be submitted to arbitration at the request of either party. By the Commonhold and Leasehold Reform Act, the effect of these clauses is limited, because the results will not be binding so far as the First Tier Tribunal is concerned. If, however, once a dispute has arisen, the parties to agree to submit it to an agreed arbitrator, they are bound by the result, which is enforceable by the courts. If such a 'post-dispute' arbitration finds that the leaseholder is in breach, this is equivalent to a finding by the First Tier Tribunal and will (if the other requirements are met) allow the freeholder to proceed with forfeiture. Arbitration may be a useful mechanism in some cases, and it may be cheaper and quicker than legal action, but it may be difficult to find an arbitrator in whom both parties have confidence.

Obligations of Freeholders
a: Exclusive possession and quiet enjoyment
The first and most important obligation on the freeholder, without which there would be no legal lease at all, is to respect the leaseholder's rights of 'exclusive possession' and 'quiet enjoyment'. Exclusive possession is the right to occupy the property and exclude others from

it, especially the freeholder. Quiet enjoyment is another way of underlining the leaseholder's rights over the property: it means that the freeholder may not interfere with the leaseholder's use of the property provided that the terms of the lease are observed.

However, the leaseholder's right to quiet enjoyment applies only to breaches by the freeholder or the freeholder's servants such as agents or contractors. It is important to note this because the term is sometimes thought to mean that the freeholder must protect the leaseholder against any activity by anyone that interferes with his use of the property: this is not so. For example, if the freeholder carries out some activity elsewhere in the building that interferes with the leaseholder, the leaseholder's right to quiet enjoyment has been breached and he is entitled to redress unless the freeholder can show that the activity was necessary, for instance to comply with repairing obligations under the lease. But if the interference is caused by someone else, perhaps another leaseholder, the freeholder's obligation to provide quiet enjoyment has not been breached. And it is worth stressing in this connection that even if the other leaseholder is in breach of his lease, it is entirely up to the freeholder whether or not to take action: other leaseholders have no power to force the freeholder to deal with the situation.

This means that if one leaseholder is breaking his lease by holding noisy parties late at night, the other leaseholders may ask, but may not require, the freeholder to take action to enforce the lease. They may, however, take legal action directly against the offending leaseholder for nuisance.

b: The 'section 48' notice

Another important protection for leaseholders is found in section 48 of the Landlord and Tenant Act 1987. This was designed to deal with the situation in which freeholders seek to avoid their responsibilities by (to put it bluntly) doing a disappearing act. Sometimes freeholders would provide no address or telephone number or other means of contact, meaning that leaseholders were unable to hold the freeholder to his side of the agreement. Sections 47 and 48 therefore lay down that the freeholder must formally notify the leaseholder of his name and give an address within England and Wales at which he can be contacted, and that this information must be repeated on every demand for rent or service charge. This has proved especially valuable for leaseholders where the freeholder lives abroad, or is a company based abroad. It should be noted that the address does not have to be the freeholder's home, nor, if the freeholder is a company, its registered office; often it will be the address of a solicitor or property management company, or simply an accommodation address. But the key point is that any notice, or legal writ, is validly served if sent to that address, and the freeholder is not allowed to claim that it never came to his notice.

It is not necessary for the notice required by section 48 to be given in a separate document; it is enough if the name and address is clearly given as part of some other document such as a service charge demand. But if the necessary notice is not given, no payment of rent, service charge, or anything else is due to the freeholder; the leaseholder may lawfully withhold it until section 48 is complied with. But leaseholders withholding payments on this ground must be careful; once the notice is given, it has retrospective effect, so that all the money due to the freeholder then becomes due immediately. Any leaseholder withholding money on the grounds that section 48 has not been complied with should, therefore, make sure that he has the money easily available so that he can pay up if he has to.

c: Good management

The freeholder is under an obligation to ensure that his management responsibilities are carried out in a proper and appropriate way. Leaseholders can challenge the freeholder in court or at the FTT if they believe they can show that they are not receiving the standard of management to which they are entitled. This may be an expensive and lengthy process but it better than the alternative, sometimes resorted to by leaseholders, of withholding rent or service charge. This is risky because, whatever the shortcomings of the freeholder's management, it puts the leaseholders in breach of the conditions of their lease and, as such, demonstrably in the wrong (even if the freeholder may be in the wrong as well).

Withholding due payments is therefore not recommended unless the freeholder is so clearly at fault that arguably no payment is due - for instance, if the service being charged for has clearly not been provided at all (as opposed to being provided inadequately), or if there has been no 'section 48' notice (see above). If leaseholders choose to withhold payment, they are strongly advised to keep the money readily to hand so that they can pay up at once if the freeholder rectifies the problem; the danger otherwise is that they will be taken to court and required to pay immediately to avoid forfeiture (see below).

Powers of Leaseholders over Management

If leaseholders want a scrutiny of the standards of management of their flats, they have power under the Leasehold Reform, Housing and Urban Development Act 1993 to demand a management audit by an auditor acting on behalf of at least two-thirds of the qualifying leaseholders. Qualifying leaseholders are those with leases of residential property originally granted for 21 years or more and requiring them to contribute to the cost of services.

The purpose of the audit, the costs of which must be met by the leaseholders demanding it, is to discover whether the freeholder's duties are being carried out efficiently and effectively. The auditor is appointed by the leaseholders and must be either a qualified accountant or a qualified surveyor and must not live in the block concerned. The auditor has the right to demand papers from the freeholder and can go to court if they are not produced.

Leaseholders' Right to Manage

Leaseholders with long leases (those originally granted for 21 years or more) also have the right to take over management of their block if they wish. This applies to blocks of two or more flats (five or more if there is a resident landlord) and no substantial non-residential part. It does not apply if the freeholder is a local authority.

The leaseholders must first form a 'Right to Manage' company ('RtM' company), which is a limited company whose membership is confined to leaseholders and the freeholder. Before seeking to take over management the RtM company must advise all leaseholders of its intention and invite them to participate. Fourteen days after this invitation, and provided the RtM company includes at least half the eligible tenants (or both, if only two are eligible), it can serve a claim notice on the landlord (or on the First Tier Tribunal if the landlord is untraceable) giving at least four months' notice of its intention to take over the management. The landlord has a month to serve a counter-notice objecting to the claim, in which case the LVT will adjudicate. If no counter-notice is served, or if the LVT so decides, the RtM company duly takes over management.

The landlord must bring to an end as quickly as possible any existing management arrangements applying to the block. The RtM company takes over the landlord's management functions, including services, repairs, maintenance, improvements, and insurance. The landlord retains its role in respect of any flats without long leaseholders (for example, those let on assured tenancies), and continues to deal with forfeiture (for more on forfeiture see the section below 'If the lease is breached'). Essentially the RtM company steps into the landlord's shoes so far as management is concerned, and it is responsible to both the landlord and the individual leaseholders for the proper carrying out of its functions.

Many leases require the landlord's approval before certain things can be done, such as assigning the lease or sub-letting. The RtM company takes over this function from the landlord, but must consult the landlord before granting approval. If the landlord objects, the matter is referred to the LVT. It seems, however, that refusal of consent by the RtM is final and cannot be challenged by the landlord (although it might be challenged by the leaseholder in question on the ground that the relevant term of the lease is unenforceable). The RtM company has authority to enforce covenants in the lease, but not by means of forfeiture.

At first blush the power to take over management in this way may appear attractive. However, leaseholders should think very carefully before they commit themselves; there are some potential snags.

The biggest problem is one of enforcement. So long as all leaseholders are agreed about what needs to be done, and are all willing and able to meet their obligations (including that of paying for services), enforcement will not be an issue and all will be well. But if some individual leaseholders refuse to pay their share, or fail to abide by the covenants in their leases, the RtM company will have to act to enforce the leases and this may well be difficult. In the first place, any steps to enforce leases will pit neighbour against neighbour and are virtually certain to cause animosity in the block. Secondly, the powerful tool of forfeiture, or threatened forfeiture, is denied to a RtM company. Finally, the RtM company, unlike most freeholders, will not have any substantial financial resources that would allow it to pursue lengthy legal action against individual leaseholders.

There are other issues. The RtM company will depend on the voluntary efforts of its members, and experience shows that many people are not willing to put in the time and effort involved in attending meetings and carrying out essential administration. RtM companies have to operate under a special constitution laid down by the Government; the aim of this is to guarantee all leaseholders' rights to be involved, but because the constitution is a standard document applying to all cases it is likely that many leaseholders will find it clumsy and inflexible. Finally, there is the question of continuing relations with the freeholder, which will expect its interests as ultimate owner to be respected by the RtM company.

In short, leaseholders contemplating the formation of a RtM company need to be sure that they are committed not only for the immediate effort of setting it up but for the long haul of carrying out management in the future. They should also recognise that, no matter how united everyone may be to start with, sooner or later the issue of enforcement will rear its head. They should certainly get legal advice about their new responsibilities before committing themselves.

The law allows another remedy in extreme cases of mismanagement. A leaseholder can use the Landlord and Tenant Act 1987 to force the appointment of a managing agent to run the block instead of the freeholder.

The leaseholder must serve a notice telling the freeholder what the problems are and warning that unless they are put right a First Tier Tribunal will be asked to appoint a managing agent. The FTT may make such an order if it satisfied that it is 'just and convenient'; the Act mentions, as specific examples where this may apply, cases where the freeholder is in breach of obligations under the lease and cases where service charges are being levied in respect of work of a poor standard or an unnecessarily high standard. Note that the procedure is not available if the freeholder is a local authority, a registered housing association, or the Crown.

Recognised Tenants' Association

A recognised tenants' association (RTA), where there is one, has additional rights to be consulted about managing agents. The RTA can serve a notice requiring the freeholder to supply details of the managing agent and the terms of the management agreement.

Leaseholders that are receiving a consistently poor or overpriced service may also wish to consider getting rid of the freeholder altogether by collective enfranchisement under the Leasehold Reform, Housing and Urban Development Act 1993.

Assignment of Leases

One of the most important characteristics of a lease - in marked contrast to most tenancies - is that it may be bought and sold. Usually, the freeholder has no say in this: the leaseholder may sell to whom he likes for the best price he can get, provided that the purchaser agrees to be bound by the terms of the lease. It is, however, usual for the lease to lay down that the freeholder must be informed of any change of leaseholder.

What actually happens when a lease is sold is that the vendor agrees to transfer to the buyer his rights and obligations under the lease. This is called 'assignment' of the lease. In some types of housing the freeholder has the right to intervene if an assignment is envisaged. The housing may, for instance, be reserved for a particular category of resident, such as the retired, so the freeholder is allowed to refuse consent to the assignment if the purchaser does not qualify.

It was mentioned above that the assignee takes over all the rights and responsibilities attaching to the lease. This means, for instance, that he takes responsibility for any arrears of service charge. This is why purchasers' solicitors go to such lengths to ensure that no arrears or other unusual obligations are outstanding.

If the Lease Is Breached

If the terms of a lease are broken, the party offended against can go to court. This may be the leaseholder, for instance if the freeholder has failed to carry out a repair. But it is normally the freeholder that takes the leaseholder to court, for failure to pay ground rent or service charges or for breach of some other requirement.

It is for the court, if satisfied that the lease has been breached, to decide what to do. The normal remedy will be that the offending party must pay compensation and that the breach (if it is still continuing) must be put right. It is also likely that the loser will be obliged to pay the winner's legal costs as well as his own, a penalty often considerably more severe that the requirement to pay compensation.

A much more severe remedy open to the freeholder if the leaseholder is in breach is forfeiture of the lease. This means what it says: the lease is forfeit to the freeholder. Forfeiture is sometimes threatened by the more aggressive class of freeholder but the good news for leaseholders is that in practice courts have shown themselves loath to grant it except in very serious cases. Since the Housing Act 1996 took effect, forfeiture for unpaid service charges has been made more difficult for freeholders; this is covered in the next Chapter.

Where forfeiture is threatened for any reason other than failure to pay rent (which, depending on the terms of the lease, may or may not include the service charge element), the freeholder must first serve a 'section 146 notice', so called after the relevant provision of the Law of Property Act 1925. In this he must state the nature of the breach of the lease, what action is required to put it right; if he wants monetary compensation for the breach, the notice must state this too.

Before the section 146 notice can be issued, it must be established that a breach of the lease has occurred. If the leaseholder has admitted the breach, the notice can be issued; otherwise, it must have been decided by a court, the FTT, or an independent arbitrator that the leaseholder is in breach. Moreover, the breach of the lease specified in the section 146 notice must have occurred during the twelve years preceding the notice. For breaches older than this, no valid section 146 notice can be served and so forfeiture is not available. If the notice is not complied with, the freeholder may proceed to forfeit; but the leaseholder may go to court for relief from forfeiture. In practice, courts have generally been willing to grant relief, but they cannot do so unless it is formally applied for. If the leaseholder, perhaps failing to realise the seriousness of the situation, fails to go to court and seek relief, the forfeiture will go ahead. If the freeholder breaches the lease, the leaseholder can go to court and seek an order requiring the freeholder to remedy the breach, to pay damages, or to do both. The commonest type of breach complained of by leaseholders is failure to carry out repairs, and this explains why action by leaseholders is less usual; they know that if they force the freeholder to do repairs the costs will be recovered through service charges. Legal action may be the best course if the dispute affects a single leaseholder; but if a number of leaseholders are involved they may well prefer to get rid of the freeholder altogether by collectively enfranchising their leases.

****

14

SERVICE CHARGES AND THE LAW

By far the commonest cause of dispute between leaseholders and freeholders is the provision of services and the levying of service charges. In extreme cases, leaseholders have been asked to contribute thousands of pounds towards the cost of major repairs, and have even suffered forfeiture of the lease if they are unable, or unwilling, to comply. Happily, such instances are rare; but even where the service charges are more moderate, they are often resented by leaseholders.

The landlord of rented property is expected to meet virtually all costs from the rent, whereas the freeholder of leasehold stock has no rent to fall back on (apart from the normally negligible ground rent). How, then, are major costs to be met when they arise? The answer, of course, is from the service charge, which is, therefore, of central importance to the management of leasehold property.

From the freeholder's point of view, the logic of service charges is impeccable. It is perfectly reasonable for freeholders to point out:

- that leaseholders benefit from the work because it has maintained or improved their homes; and
- that the fact that the work has been done means that leaseholders will get a better price when they come to sell; and
- that people that own their homes freehold have to find the money to meet costs of this kind.

In short, the purchase of a lease means the acceptance of a commitment to pay the appropriate share of costs. But this does not mean that leaseholders have no scope to challenge or query service charges. Under sections 18 to 30 of the Landlord and Tenant Act 1985, as amended by the 2002 Commonhold and Leasehold Reform Act, they have extensive legal protection against improper or unreasonable charging by freeholders, and this is discussed later in the Chapter. First, however, we should look at how a typical service charge is made up.

What goes into a Service Charge?

The lease will say how often service charges are levied: typically, monthly, six-monthly or annually. It is usual to collect the ground rent at the same time, but this is usually a fairly small component of the bill. The service charge proper will normally consist of three elements.

- **The management fee** is the charge made by the freeholder, or the freeholder's agent, to cover the administrative cost of providing the service and collecting the charge. Usually it will be much the same amount from one year to the next, but if major works have occurred the management fee will usually be higher to cover the extra costs of appointing and supervising contractors; 15% of the cost of the works is a common figure.

- **Direct costs (routine expenditure)** cover costs such as the supply of electricity to communal areas, building insurance, and the like. Again, these costs are likely to be fairly constant from year to year, so leaseholders   know in advance roughly how much they are likely to   have to pay.

- **Direct costs (exceptional expenditure)** cover costs that are likely to be irregular but heavy. They usually result from maintenance and repair, and it is because this component of the service charge is so unpredictable that it gives rise to so many problems. Where a house has been divided into leasehold flats, the freeholder's costs will usually be similar to what a normal homeowner would be obliged to pay; in other words, the costs may well be in the thousands (for a new roof, say) but are unlikely to be higher. Even so, a charge of £5000 for a new roof, even if divided between three or four flats, is still a major cost from the point of view of the individual leaseholder, especially if it is unexpected. The situation can be far worse in blocks of flats, where the costs of essential repair and maintenance may run into millions. Replacement of worn-out lifts, for example, is notoriously costly; and costs arising from structural defects are likely to be higher still.

Unreasonable Service Charges
General Principles

Sections 18 to 30 of the Landlord and Tenant Act 1985, as amended by the Landlord and Tenant Act 1987, and the Commonhold and Leasehold Reform Act 2002, grant substantial protection to leaseholders of residential property. This protection was introduced after complaints of exploitation by unscrupulous leaseholders, who were alleged to be carrying out unnecessary, or even fictitious, repairs at extravagant prices, whilst not providing the information that would have enabled leaseholders to query the bill. The effect of the Acts is to require freeholders to provide leaseholders with full information about service charges and to consult them before expensive works are carried out.

A few leases, namely those granted under the right to buy by local authorities or registered housing associations, have some additional protection under the Housing Act 1985 (see below), but sections 18 to 30 apply to all residential leases where the service charge depends on how much the freeholder spends. They set out the key rules that freeholders must observe in order to recover the cost, including overheads, of 'services, repairs, maintenance or insurance', as well as the freeholder's costs of management. It should be noted that failure by leaseholders to pay the service charge does not relieve the freeholder of the obligation to provide the services. The freeholder's remedy is to sue the leaseholder for the outstanding charges, or even to seek forfeiture of the lease (see below). Section 19 of the Landlord and Tenant Act 1985, as amended, provides the key protection to leaseholders by laying down that service charges are recoverable only if they are 'reasonably incurred' and if the services or works are of a reasonable standard. This means that the charge:

- o   must relate to some form of 'service, repair, maintenance, or insurance' that the freeholder is required to provide under the lease;
- o   - must be reasonable (that is, the landlord may not recover costs incurred unnecessarily or extravagantly);
- o   - may cover overheads and management costs only if these too are reasonable.

In addition, the charge must normally be passed on to the leaseholders within 18 months of being incurred, and in some cases the freeholder must consult leaseholders before spending the money. These points are covered below.

The Housing Act 1996 (amended by the Commonhold and Leasehold Reform Act 2002) gave leaseholders new powers to refer service charges to the Leasehold Valuation Tribunal (LVT). LVT's have been replaced by First Tier Tribunals (introduced in July 2013)

The First Tier tribunal

Leaseholders can apply to the First-tier Tribunal (Property Chamber) to deal with disputes about service charges, repairs, extending leases or buying the freehold. This Tribunal was called the Leasehold Valuation Tribunal

What disputes the tribunal deals with

If you own a leasehold flat or house and can't resolve a dispute with your freeholder, you may be able to apply to a tribunal for a decision. This tribunal can help with disputes over leasehold problems, such as:

- insuring the building
- the amount billed for service charges
- the quality of services such as cleaning and maintenance
- extending your lease
- buying the freehold

How to apply to the tribunal

The tribunal that deals with leaseholder disputes is called the First-tier Tribunal (Property Chamber). There are five regional tribunals. You can find details of your local tribunal from HM Courts & Tribunals Service. Apply to the tribunal using the correct form. This is available from Gov.uk.

Send the form to the regional tribunal that covers your area. The address is on the form. The tribunal contacts you to tell you if it can consider your case. You may be asked to provide more information. You can ask for a hearing or the case can be decided on the evidence you and the freeholder send. Find out more from Gov.uk about what happens at a tribunal hearing.

Costs of taking a case to the tribunal

You may have to pay a fee to apply to the tribunal. You can apply for an exemption or a reduced fee if you receive certain benefits or have a low income. If the problem affects more than one leaseholder, you can apply together and share the costs. You may have to pay a surveyor, property manager or a solicitor. In limited cases the tribunal can order the freeholder to compensate you.

If you win the case, the tribunal may be able to order the freeholder to refund your application fee. Some freeholders can include their legal costs in your service charge bill. Check your lease to see if this is allowed.

The tribunal's decision

The tribunal's decision is binding on you and the freeholder. You might need to take court action to recover any money your freeholder owes you.

What the tribunal can decide

Disputes about service charges

The tribunal can consider if a service charge is payable, and if so how much you must pay.

Disputes about repairs

The tribunal can change what your lease says about maintenance and repairs if what's said is unclear or doesn't cover the issue in dispute.

Disputes about poor management

The tribunal can appoint a new manager if you can prove your building is being badly managed. The freeholder would still own the property but would lose the right to manage it.

Lease extension disputes

The tribunal can set a price for extending your lease or buying the freehold if you and the freeholder haven't been able to agree.

Appeals against the tribunal's decision

You may be able to appeal against the tribunal's decision. You can usually only do this if the tribunal has acted unfairly or didn't follow the correct procedures. You can't appeal because you don't like the tribunal's decision.

Service Charge demands

Section 153 of the 2002 Commonhold and Leasehold Reform Act states that all demands for service charges must be accompanied by a summary of leaseholders rights and obligations. Accordingly, a leaseholder can withhold payment of charges if such a summary is not contained with a demand. Where a tenant withholds charges under section 153, the sections of a lease pertaining to payment of charges will not apply for the period for which the charge is withheld.

Sample summary of rights and obligations

Service Charges - Summary of tenants' rights and obligations

1. This summary, which briefly sets out your rights and obligations in relation to variable service charges, must by law accompany a demand for service charges. Unless a summary is sent to you with a demand, you may withhold the service charge. The summary does not give a full interpretation of the law and if you are in any doubt about your rights and obligations you should seek independent advice.

2. Your lease sets out your obligations to pay service charges to your landlord in addition to your rent. Service charges are amounts payable for services, repairs, maintenance, improvements, insurance or the landlord's costs of management, to the extent that the costs have been reasonably incurred.

3. You have the right to ask a First Tier Tribunal to determine whether you are liable to pay service charges for services, repairs, maintenance, improvements, insurance or management. You may make a request before or after you have paid the service charge. If the tribunal determines that the service charge is payable, the tribunal may also determine-

    o who should pay the service charge and who it should be paid to;

- o the amount;
- o the date it should be paid by; and
- o how it should be paid.

However, you do not have these rights where-
- o a matter has been agreed or admitted by you;
- o a matter has already been, or is to be, referred to arbitration or has been determined by arbitration and you agreed to go to arbitration after the disagreement about the service charge or costs arose; or a matter has been decided by a court.

4. If your lease allows your landlord to recover costs incurred or that may be incurred in legal proceedings as service charges, you may ask the court or tribunal, before which those proceedings were brought, to rule that your landlord may not do so.

5. Where you seek a determination from a First Tier tribunal, you will have to pay an application fee and, where the matter proceeds to a hearing, a hearing fee, unless you qualify for a waiver or reduction. The total fees payable will not exceed £500, but making an application may incur additional costs, such as professional fees, which you may also have to pay.

6. A First Tier tribunal has the power to award costs, against a party to any proceedings where-
- o it dismisses a matter because it is frivolous, vexatious or an abuse of process; or
- o it considers a party has acted frivolously, vexatiously, abusively, disruptively or unreasonably.
- o The Upper Tribunal (Lands Chamber) has similar powers when hearing an appeal against a decision of a First Tier Tribunal.

7. If your landlord-

o   proposes works on a building or any other premises that will cost you or any other tenant more than £250, or

o   proposes to enter into an agreement for works or services which will last for more than 12 months and will cost you or any other tenant more than £100 in any 12 month accounting period,

then your contribution will be limited to these amounts unless your landlord has properly consulted on the proposed works or agreement or a First Tier Tribunal has agreed that consultation is not required. You have the right to apply to the First Tier tribunal to ask it to determine whether your lease should be varied on the grounds that it does not make satisfactory provision in respect of the calculation of a service charge payable under the lease.

8.   You have the right to write to your landlord to request a written summary of the costs which make up the service charges. The summary must-

o   cover the last 12 month period used for making up the accounts relating to the service charge ending no later than the date of your request, where the accounts are made up for 12 month periods; or

o   cover the 12 month period ending with the date of your request, where the accounts are not made up for 12 month periods.

o   The summary must be given to you within 1 month of your request or 6 months of the end of the period to which the summary relates whichever is the later.

9.   You have the right, within 6 months of receiving a written summary of costs, to require the landlord to provide you with reasonable facilities to inspect the accounts, receipts and other documents supporting the summary and for taking copies or extracts from them.

10. You have the right to ask an accountant or surveyor to carry out an audit of the financial management of the premises containing your dwelling, to establish the obligations of your landlord and the extent to which the service charges you pay are being used efficiently. It will depend on your circumstances whether you can exercise this right alone or only with the support of others living in the premises. You are strongly advised to seek independent advice before exercising this right.

11. Your lease may give your landlord a right of re-entry or forfeiture where you have failed to pay charges which are properly due under the lease. However, to exercise this right, the landlord must meet all the legal requirements and obtain a court order. A court order will only be granted if you have admitted you are liable to pay the amount or it is finally determined by a court, tribunal or by arbitration that the amount is due. The court has a wide discretion in granting such an order and it will take into account all the circumstances of the case.

Consultation with Leaseholders

Section 20 of the LTA 1985, which is the area of the Act dealing with the landlords obligation to consult leaseholders over both major expenditure, and also long-term agreements for the provision of services, has been substituted by section 151 of the 2002 Commonhold and Leasehold Reform Act.

Major works and long term agreements

Section 151 provides extra protection where the cost of works is more than £250 per leaseholder. Therefore, if a landlord owns a block of 20 flats and wishes to spend £8,000 on repairs, the limit above which he will have to legally consult is £5,000. Costs above this level are irrecoverable (except, sometimes, when the works are urgent) unless the freeholder has taken steps to inform and consult tenants. If the leaseholders are represented by a recognised tenants' association, i.e. formally constituted and recognised by the landlord as well as leaseholders, they must also receive copies of the consultation notices along with individual leaseholders.

In relation to long term agreements, these are agreements over 12 months. Such agreements may be those for servicing lifts. They do not include contracts of employment. The consultation limit for long term contracts is now £100 per person per annum. If the amount exceeds this then consultation must be carried out. The steps in the consultation procedure are as follows:

Landlords statement of why works are necessary. There is a requirement for the landlord to state why he considers the works or the agreement to be necessary. This is defined by a 1-month period within which the landlord must take account of all responses from leaseholders. All letters and responses have to be prepared in accordance with the requirements of the Act (2002 CLRA).

Estimates. Following this initial stage, at least two estimates must be obtained, of which at least one must be from someone wholly unconnected with the freeholder (obviously a building firm that the freeholder owns or works for is not 'wholly unconnected'; nor is the freeholder's managing agent).

Notification to leaseholders The freeholder must either display a copy of the estimates somewhere they are likely to be seen by everyone liable to pay the service charge, or (preferably) send copies to everyone liable to pay the service charge.

Consultation The notification must describe the works to be carried out and must seek comments and observations, giving a deadline for replies and an address in the UK to which they may be sent. The deadline must be at least a month after the notice was sent or displayed.

Freeholder's response The freeholder must 'have regard' to any representations received. This does not mean, of course, that the freeholder must do what the leaseholders say. It does mean, however, that the freeholder must consider any comments received, and good freeholders often demonstrate that they have done so by sending a reasoned reply.

Therefore, a consultation period will usually be a minimum of 60 days from notification to instructions to carry out works.

If a service charge is challenged in court for failure to follow these procedures, it is a defence for the freeholder to show that the works were urgent. However, the court would need to be satisfied that the urgency was genuine and that the freeholder behaved reasonably in the circumstances.

Section 151 is important because it gives the leaseholders notification of any unusual items in the offing and gives them an opportunity to raise any concerns and objections. If the leaseholder has any reservations at all, it is vital that they be put before the freeholder at this stage. It is highly unlikely, in the event of legal action later, that the court will support a leaseholder who raised no objection until the bill arrived. It is common for freeholders and their agents to fail to comply with the requirements of section 151. This comment applies not only where the freehold is owned by an individual or a relatively small organisation (where mistakes might be more understandable) but also where the freeholder is a large, well resourced body like a local authority. As a result leaseholders are often paying service charges that are not due, so all leaseholders should, before paying a service charge containing unusual items, ensure that section 151, if it applies, has been scrupulously followed. If not, they can refuse to pay.

Other Protection for Leaseholders

Grant-aided works:

If the freeholder has received a grant towards the cost of carrying out the works, the amount must be deducted from the service charge levied on leaseholders.

Late charging

Service charge bills may not normally include costs incurred more than eighteen months earlier. The freeholder may, however, notify leaseholders within the eighteen month period that they will have to pay a certain cost, and then bill them later. This might happen if, for instance, the freeholder is in dispute with a contractor about the level of a bill or the standard of work.

Pre-charging

Sometimes a lease will contain a provision allowing the freeholder to make a charge to cover future costs besides those already incurred. This practice, which is perfectly lawful in itself, may be in the interests of the leaseholders by spreading over a longer period the cost of major works. It is, however, subject to the same requirement of reasonableness.

Court costs

Section 20C of the LTA 1985, provides protection against a specific abuse of the service charge system by freeholders. Previously, freeholders tended to regard their legal costs as part of the process of managing the housing and thus as recoverable from leaseholders. Such an attitude is not necessarily unreasonable. For example, if the freeholder is suing a builder for poor work, he is, in effect, acting on behalf of all the leaseholders and it is fair that they should pay any legal costs. But suppose the freeholder were involved in legal proceedings against one of the leaseholders: if the leaseholder lost, he would probably be ordered to pay the freeholder's costs as well as his own; but if the freeholder lost, and had to pay both his own and the leaseholder's costs, he could simply, under the previous law, recover the money as part of the management element in the service charge. This meant that the freeholder was able to pursue legal action against leaseholders without fear of heavy legal costs in the event of defeat, the very factor that deters most people from resorting to law.

To prevent this, section 20C allows leaseholders to seek an order that the freeholder's legal costs must not be counted towards service charges. Such an order is available in respect of not only court proceedings but also proceedings before a First Tier Tribunal Tribunal, the Lands Tribunal, or an arbitral tribunal. An application for an order may be made by the leaseholder concerned in the case to the court or tribunal hearing it. If the case has finished, any leaseholder may apply for an order to the Lands Tribunal if the case was heard there, to any Leasehold Tribunal if it was heard by a LT, or otherwise to the county court.

Service charges held on trust

Section 42 of the Landlord and Tenant Act 1987 (as amended by the 2002 CLRA) further strengthened the position of leaseholders by laying down that the freeholder, or the freeholder's agent, must hold service charge monies in a suitable trust fund that will ensure that the money is protected and cannot be seized by the freeholder's creditors if the freeholder goes bankrupt or into liquidation. However, public sector freeholders, notably local authorities and registered housing associations, are exempt from this requirement.

Insurance

Usually the lease provides for the landlord to arrange the insurance of the building (not the contents) and charge the cost as a service charge. This is the normal arrangement for buildings divided into flats, since it is important that there should be one single policy covering all risks to the building as a whole. It is normally recovered as part of the service charges and therefore the cost of the insurance may be challenged before or verified by the LVT in the usual way.

Where a service charge consists of or includes an amount payable for insurance, an individual leaseholder or the secretary of a recognised tenants' association may ask the landlord for a written summary of the policy or an opportunity to inspect and take copies of the policy.

The request must be made in writing and the landlord must comply within 21 days of receiving it. Where the request is for a written summary, the summary must show:
– the sum for which the property is insured;
– the name of the insurer;
– the risks covered in the policy.

The landlord can only be required to provide the summary once in each insurance period (usually a year).

Where the request is for sight of the policy, the landlord must provide reasonable access for inspection of the policy and any other relevant documents which provide evidence of payment, including receipts, and facilities for copying them. Alternatively, the request may be for the landlord to provide the copies of the policy and specified documents himself and to send them to the leaseholder or association or arrange for them to be collected.

'Period of Grace'

When a dwelling is sold under the right to buy by a local authority or non-charitable housing association, the purchaser is given an estimate of service charges for the following five years. This estimate is the maximum recoverable during that time. Some purchasers under the right to buy have, however, had a very rude shock when the five year period of grace expires - see *Exceptionally High Service Charges* below.

The role of a recognised tenants' association

The tenants who are liable to pay for the provision of services may, if they wish, form a recognised tenants' association (RTA) under section 29 of the Landlord and Tenant Act 1985. Note that leaseholders count as tenants for this purpose (see Chapter One, where it explained that legally the two terms are interchangeable). If the freeholder refuses to give a notice recognising the RTA, it may apply for recognition to any member of the local Rent Assessment Committee panel. An important benefit of having a RTA is that it has the right, at the beginning of the consultation process, to recommend persons or organisations that should be invited to submit estimates. However, the freeholder is under no obligation to accept these recommendations.

Another advantage is that the RTA can, whether the freeholder likes it or not, appoint a qualified surveyor to advise on matters relating to service charges. The surveyor has extensive rights to inspect the freeholder's documentation and take copies, and can enforce these rights in court if necessary.

Statement of accounts to leaseholders

Under section 152 of the Commonhold and Leasehold Reform Act 2002, which has substituted s.21 of the Landlord and Tenant Act 1985, a landlord must supply a statement of accounts to each tenant by who service charges are payable, in relation to each accounting period. These accounts deal with:

a. Service charges of the tenant and the tenants of dwellings associated with his dwelling
b. Relevant costs relating to those service charges
c. The aggregate amount standing to the credit of the tenant and the tenants of those dwellings at the beginning and the end of the accounting period in question.

This statement of account must be supplied to the tenant not later than six months after the accounting period. A certificate of a qualified auditor must be supplied and, in addition, a summary of the rights and obligations of the tenant in relation to service charges must be supplied.

Challenging Service Charges

The Landlord and Tenant Act not only allows leaseholders to take action against unreasonable behaviour by the freeholder; it also enables them to take the initiative. This is done in two ways: by giving leaseholders rights to demand information, and by allowing them to challenge the reasonableness of the charge.

Right to require information

Leaseholders have the right to ask freeholders for a written summary of costs counting towards the service charge. This is contained within s.22 of the Landlord and Tenant Act 1985, as amended by s.154 of the Commonhold and Leasehold Reform Act 2002. Such a summary must cover either the twelve months up to the point where it was requested or, if accounts are drawn up annually, the last complete twelve-month accounting period before the request was made. It must be sent to the leaseholder within 21 days of the request or within six months of the end of the period it covers, whichever is the later. Failure to provide it without reasonable excuse is a criminal offence carrying a maximum fine of £2500.

The law lays down some minimum requirements for the summary. It must:

- o cover all the costs incurred during the twelve months it covers, even if they were included in service charge bills of an earlier or later period (see above for late charging and pre-charging);
- o show how the costs incurred by the freeholder are reflected in

the service charges paid, or to be paid, by leaseholders;

- o say whether it includes any work covered by a grant (see above);
- o distinguish: (a) those costs incurred for which the freeholder was not billed during the period; (b) those for which he was billed and did not pay; (c) those for which he paid bills.

If it covers five or more dwellings, the summary must, in addition, be certified by a qualified accountant as being a fair summary, complying with the Act, and supported by appropriate documentation. The purpose of section 22, as amended, is to put leaseholders in a position to challenge their service charges. After receiving the summary, the leaseholder has six months in which to ask the freeholder to make facilities available so that he can inspect the documents supporting the summary (bills, receipts, and so on) and take copies or extracts. The freeholder must respond within a month and make the facilities available within the two months following that; the inspection itself must be free, although the freeholder can make a reasonable charge for the copies and extracts. Failure to provide these facilities, like failure to supply the summary, is punishable by a fine of up to £2500.

Very similar rules apply where the lease allows, or requires, the freeholder to take out insurance against certain contingencies, such as major repair, and to recover the premiums through the service charge. This is not unreasonable in itself and will, indeed, often be in the interests of leaseholders. The danger is, however, that the freeholder, knowing that the premiums are, in effect, being paid by someone else, has no incentive to shop around for the best deal. Section 30A of the Landlord and Tenant Act 1985 therefore lays down that leaseholders, or the secretary of the recognised tenants' association if there is one, may ask the freeholder for information about the policy. Failure to supply it, or to make facilities to inspect relevant documents available if requested to do so, is an offence incurring a fine of up to £2500.

Challenging the reasonableness of a service charge

Any leaseholder liable to pay a service charge, and for that matter any freeholder levying one, may refer the charge to a First Tier Tribunal to determine its reasonableness. This may be done at any time, even when the service in question is merely a proposal by the freeholder (for instance, for future major works). But the FTT will not consider a service charge if:

- it has already been approved by a court; or
- if the leaseholder has agreed to refer it to arbitration; or
- if the leaseholder has agreed it.

The first of these exceptions is obvious and the second is unlikely to apply very often. The third one is the problem: leaseholders should be careful, in their dealings with freeholders, to say or do nothing that could be taken to imply that they agree with any service charge that is in any way doubtful.

The FTT will consider:

o whether the freeholder's costs of services, repairs, maintenance, insurance, or management are reasonably incurred;

o whether the services or works are of a reasonable standard; and

o whether any payment required in advance is reasonable.

The fees for application to a FTT can be obtained from the FTT and will usually change annually. Appeal against a FTT decision is not to the courts but to the Lands Tribunal.

By section 19 of the Landlord and Tenant Act 1985, any service charge deemed unreasonable by the FTT is irrecoverable by the freeholder. The determination of service charges by the FTT also plays an important part in the rules governing the use of forfeiture to recover service charges. .

Forfeiture for Unpaid Service Charges

Forfeiture was mentioned at the end of Chapter Two. Briefly, it is the right of the freeholder to take possession of the property if the leaseholder breaches the lease.

By section 81 of the Housing Act 1996, as amended by the 2002 Commonhold and Leasehold Reform Act, forfeiture for an unpaid service charge is available to the freeholder only if:

- the leaseholder has agreed the charge; or
- the charge has been upheld through arbitration or by a court or First Tier Tribunal.

Regarding the first of these, it is necessary only to reiterate the warning to leaseholders to say or do nothing that could possibly be construed as representing their agreement to any service charge about whose legitimacy they have the slightest doubt.

Regarding the second, it should be noted that where the leaseholder has not agreed the service charge, court proceedings or formal arbitration are necessary before the freeholder can forfeit the lease.

Exceptionally High Service Charges

So far this Chapter has focused on service charges of normal proportions that, however unforeseen and unwelcome they may be, should be within the means of the great majority of leaseholders. A minority of leaseholders, however, face the much more serious problem of consistently very high service charges. Where the cause is sharp practice by the freeholder, or failure to observe the legal requirements, the leaseholder can look for protection to the Landlord and Tenant Act as described above. Often, however, the freeholder is not to blame:

rather, the problem is that the work is genuinely necessary and unavoidably expensive. In this situation, and provided the landlord carefully follows the procedures laid down, the Landlord and Tenant Act offers no protection.

****

15

BUYING A FREEHOLD AND EXTENDING A LEASE

LEASEHOLD REFORM, HOUSING AND URBAN DEVELOPMENT ACT 1993

The area of leasehold enfranchisement has attracted a plethora of media and academic interest since its formal introduction in 1967 and has been amended and expanded over the past four decades. The right of long leaseholders to buy their landlord's interest outright or acquire an extended lease term, is unique to England and Wales and, perhaps unsurprisingly, has led to a number of legal challenges over the years. Landlords and tenants alike are anxious to protect their respective property interests in a market that shows no sign of abating. Consequently, this area of the law is continually evolving.

In general terms, the legislation confers two distinct rights: to purchase the freehold, either individually in relation to leasehold houses, or collectively for a block of flats, or to seek a lease extension. Although these rights are curtailed by the statutory tests for qualification, changes to the legislation, introduced by the Commonhold and Leasehold Reform Act 2002, have made it easier than ever for leaseholders to make a claim.

The requirement that leaseholders must have occupied the property in question for a period of two years (the so-called residence requirement) has largely been swept away and replaced by a new, two year ownership test. Indeed, in the case of a collective enfranchisement, even the ownership requirement has been removed. Likewise, qualification tests based on the property's ratable values and rent have gone, with the result that higher value houses, for example, may now enfranchise.

The Collective Right to enfranchise
What is it?
This gives the right for tenants of flats acting together to purchase the freehold and any headleases of their building. In order for the building to qualify under the Act, it must:
• be an independent building or be a part of a building which is   capable of independent development; and
• contain two or more flats held by qualifying tenants; and
• have at least two thirds of the flats held by qualifying tenants.
In order to be a qualifying tenant you must have a long lease which means a lease which, when originally granted, was for a term of more than 21 years. However, you must not own three or more flats in the building. You cannot be a qualifying tenant if you hold a business lease.

Notwithstanding the above, the building will not qualify if:
• it comprises four or less units and has a "resident freeholder";
• more than 25% of the internal floor space (excluding common parts) is used for non-residential purposes;
• the building is part of an operational railway.

How do I prepare for a claim?
Any qualifying tenant can give a notice to his landlord or the managing agent requiring details of the various legal interests in the block. This notice places no commitment on the tenant but the response to the notice should provide the tenant with the information necessary for him to ascertain whether the building contains a sufficient number of qualifying tenants for it to qualify.

Having established that the building qualifies, it is then advisable to ascertain whether you have a sufficient number of tenants who want to participate, both for the purpose of qualifying for enfranchisement and for the purpose of being able to finance the acquisition. In order to qualify for enfranchisement, you need to establish that the number of participating tenants comprises not less than one half of all the flats in the building.

However, if there are only two flats in the building then both must participate.

When you have established that the building qualifies and that there is a sufficient number of qualifying tenants who wish to participate, then there are five further practical steps which should be taken before embarking on the enfranchisement procedure.

First, you need to establish what it is going to cost by obtaining a valuation. In simple terms, the price to be paid by the participating tenants to purchase the freehold of the building is the aggregate of:

- The building's investment value to the freeholder-the capitalised value of his ground rents and the value of his reversion (being the present freehold vacant possession value deferred for the unexpired term of the lease).

- One half of the marriage value-the increased value attributable to the freehold by virtue of the participating tenants being able to grant themselves extended leases at nil premium and a peppercorn rent. The marriage value attributable to a lease held by a participating tenant will be deemed to be nil if that lease has an unexpired term of more than 80 years at the date that the initial notice is given.

- Compensation for loss of value of other property owned by the freeholder, including development value consequent to the severance of the building from that other property.

The valuation date is the date that the claim notice is given. Value added to the flat of a participating tenant by tenant's improvements is disregarded in the valuation.

For the purposes of calculating price, the tenants should take the advice of a properly qualified surveyor or valuer with experience in the field of enfranchisement and knowledge of the market.

In addition to the price and the participating tenants' own legal costs and valuation fees, the claimants will be required to reimburse the freeholder his legal costs and valuation fees.

Secondly, the participators will need to establish how to finance the cost of acquisition. It may, for example, be necessary for a number of participating tenants to seek a further advance from a Building Society or Bank. In particular, the participators will want to decide who is to finance the purchase of the non-participators' flats and on what basis.

Thirdly, it will be necessary to establish what vehicle the participating tenants should use in order to buy the freehold and how they will establish and regulate the relationship between themselves. In most cases, this is likely to be through a company structure, although in some circumstances a trust might be more appropriate. It should be noted that the participating tenants do not all have to have equal shares, so that the proportion of the shareholdings will be a matter for negotiation between them.

The 2002 Act provides for collective claims to be made through the mechanism of a Right to Enfranchise (RTE) company. However those provisions have never been brought into force and it is unlikely that they will be.

Fourthly, the participating tenants should seek advice to establish whether there are tax implications to the transaction, both in relation to their individual positions and in relation to the vehicle chosen to buy the freehold.

Finally, the collective enfranchisement legislation provides no guidance or controls on the way in which the participating tenants should work together in order to acquire the freehold. Since the purchase may well involve substantial sums of money and is likely to take time to complete and, during this time, the participating tenants will be heavily reliant on each other for the performance of tasks within strict limits, it is strongly advised that, before embarking on a claim, the participating tenants should enter into a formal agreement (called a participation agreement) in order to regulate the relationship between them during the course of the claim.

How is the claim made?

It is important to be aware that most of the time limits imposed on the procedural stages of the claim are strict and a failure to do something within the required time frame can have dire consequences for the defaulter. It is therefore essential that, by the time you reach the next stage of the procedure, you are well organised and backed by expert professional advice.

The reason for this is that the next procedural step is the service by the participating tenants on the landlord of what the Act calls the initial notice – the notice which claims the right to collective enfranchisement. Costs start to run against the tenants from the time they serve the initial notice. Amongst other things this notice must specify:

• the extent of the property to be acquired – supported by a plan;
• full particulars of all the qualifying tenants in the building – not just the participating tenants;
• the price being offered for the freehold – the offer should be genuine;
• the name and address of the nominee purchaser – the person or company nominated by the participating tenants to conduct the negotiations and to buy the freehold on their behalf;
• the date by which the freeholder must give his counter-notice, being a date not less than two months from the date of the service of the initial notice.

The freeholder is likely to respond with a procedural notice requiring the participating tenants to deduce title. The freeholder's valuer is also likely to inspect the building for the purpose of carrying out a valuation.

Within the period specified in the initial notice, the freeholder must serve his counter-notice. First and foremost, this must state whether or not the claim is admitted. If it is not, then the participating tenants must decide if they wish to dispute the rejection through the courts.

There are circumstances where the freeholder can resist a claim on the ground of redevelopment.

If the claim is admitted, then the counter-notice must state, amongst other things:

• which of the proposals contained in the initial notice are acceptable;
• which of the proposals contained in the initial notice are not acceptable and what are the freeholder's counter-proposals –particularly on price;
• whether the freeholder wants a leaseback on any units in the building not held by a qualifying tenant (for example, a flat subject to a short term tenancy or a commercial unit).
• compensation for loss in value of other property owned by the freeholder, including development value consequent to sale

Disputes

If any terms of acquisition (including the price) remain in dispute after two months following the date of the counter-notice, then either party can apply to the leasehold valuation tribunal for the matter in dispute to be determined.

This application must be made within six months following the date of the counter-notice or the claim is lost. Most claims are settled by negotiation. If a First Tier Tribunal is required to make a determination, then there is a right to appeal that decision to the Lands Tribunal if permission is given to do so.

Completion

Once the terms of acquisition have been agreed or determined by the FTT tribunal, then the matter reverts to a conveyancing transaction with the parties entering into a sale contract on the terms agreed or determined and thence to completion.

If the matter proceeds to completion, then the participating tenants, through their nominee purchaser, will become the freeholder of the building, subject to the various flat leases. In effect, the participating tenants will replace the existing freeholder. This will put them in a position to grant themselves extended leases.

There may be taxation consequences on granting an extended lease, particularly for second home owners. There will also be responsibilities. The participating tenants will become responsible for the management of the building and the administration of the service charge account in accordance with the covenants in the original leases.

If the nominee purchaser is a company, all participators will be shareholders and some will be officers of that company. These are all matters on which clear professional advice will be needed. It is important to note that an individual tenant has no right to become a participating tenant – even if he is a qualifying tenant. It is a matter for the tenants to resolve between themselves. You can always ask to be allowed to join in, but you will have no remedy if refused. If a group does form without you – and does not need you – you may well find yourself left out.

However, if you are left out, that need not necessarily be the end of the road. This is because of the second major innovation that was introduced by the 1993 Act – the individual right to acquire a new lease.

The individual right to extend leases
What is it?
The individual right to a statutory lease extension applies to all qualifying tenants of flats. The condition is that you must be the tenant of a flat which you hold on a long lease (i.e. a lease for an original term in excess of 21 years). Furthermore, you must have owned the lease for at least two years before the date of the claim. For the purpose of the lease extension, There is no limit to the number of flats you may own in the building and you may extend any or all of them provided that the conditions are met. However, you cannot be a qualifying tenant if you hold a business lease.

Prior to the 2002 Act, the personal representatives of a deceased tenant had no rights to make a claim, even where the deceased tenant was able to fulfil the qualifying conditions. However, such personal representatives can now make a claim provided that the right is exercised within a period of two years from the date of grant of probate.

What do I get?

If you qualify, then you will be entitled to acquire a new extended lease in substitution for your existing lease. This extended lease will be for a term expiring 90 years after the end of the current lease and will reserve a peppercorn rent throughout the term.

Broadly, the lease will otherwise be on the same terms as the existing lease but the landlord will have certain additional redevelopment rights, exercisable within 12 months before the expiration of the current lease term and within 5 years before the expiration of the extended lease.

The price

The price to be paid for the new lease will be the aggregate of:

• the diminution in value of the landlord's interest in the flat, consequent on the grant of the extended lease; being the capitalised value of the landlord's ground rent and the value of his reversion (being the present near-freehold vacant possession value deferred for the unexpired lease term);
• 50% of the marriage value (the additional value released by the tenant's ability to merge the extended lease with the existing lease) must be paid to the landlord although the marriage value will be deemed to be nil if the existing lease has an unexpired term of more than 80 years at the date of the claim;
• compensation for loss in value of other property owned by the freeholder, including development value, consequent on the grant of the new lease
.

The valuation date is the date of the claim notice. In addition to the price and the tenant's own legal costs and valuation fees, you will also be required to reimburse the freeholder his legal costs and valuation fees.

How do I claim?

The procedure to be followed is very similar to that for collective enfranchisement. It is therefore important to be aware that most of the time limits imposed on the procedural stages of the claim are strict and a failure to do something within the required time frame can have dire consequences for the defaulter.

The qualifying tenant can serve a preliminary notice to obtain information. Thereafter, he serves his notice of claim (in this case called the tenant's notice of claim) which amongst other things needs to state:

• a description of the flat – but not necessarily with a plan;

• sufficient particulars to establish that the lease qualifies;

• the premium being offered – it must be a bona fide offer;

• the terms of the new lease;

• the date by which the landlord must give the counter-notice, being a date not less than two months from the date of service of the tenant's notice.

The landlord is likely to respond with a procedural notice requiring payment of a deposit (equal to 10% of the premium being offered) and asking the tenant to deduce title. The landlord's valuer is also likely to inspect the flat for the purpose of carrying out a valuation.

Within the period specified in the tenant's notice, the landlord must serve his counter-notice. First and foremost, this must state whether or not the claim is admitted. If it is not, then the tenant must decide if he wishes to dispute the rejection through the courts. However, unlike a collective enfranchisement claim where the nominee purchaser makes the application to the court in these circumstances, in the case of the statutory lease extension, it is the landlord who makes the application if he has refused the claim.

Enfranchisement

There are circumstances where the landlord can resist a claim on the ground of redevelopment. If the claim is admitted, then the counter-notice must state, amongst other things:

• which of the proposals contained in the tenant's notice are acceptable;

• which of the proposals contained in the tenant's notice are not acceptable and what are the landlord's counter-proposals – particularly the premium.

Disputes

If either the terms of the lease or the premium remain in dispute after two months following the date of the counter-notice, then either party can apply to the leasehold valuation tribunal for the matter in dispute to be determined.

This application must be made within six months following the date of the counter-notice or the claim is lost. Most claims are settled by negotiation. If a First Tier Tribunal is required to make a determination, then there is a right to appeal that decision to the Lands Tribunal if permission is given to do so

Completion

Once the terms of the lease and the premium have been agreed or determined by the FTT then the matter reverts to a conveyancing transaction with the parties proceeding to completion of the new lease.

The tenant can withdraw at any time and there are provisions for the tenant's notice to be considered withdrawn if certain strict time limits are not met by the tenant. As in collective enfranchisement, the tenant is on risk as to costs as from the date of his tenant's notice so it is essential to be prepared and to be properly advised before starting down the road to an extension.

A tenant's notice is capable of being assigned but only in conjunction with a contemporaneous assignment of the lease. It is common for a seller to serve a notice and then sell that notice with the lease to a purchaser, who will take over the claim. There is no limit to the number of times that a tenant can exercise this right – so long as he is prepared to pay the costs for doing so.

Enfranchisement of Houses-Leasehold Reform Act 1967
What is the right?

The Leasehold Reform Act 1967 gives the tenant of a leasehold house who fulfils certain rules of qualification the right to acquire the freehold and any intermediate leases.

How do I qualify?

In looking at the rules of qualification under the 1967 Act, there are three basic questions that need to be answered. First, does the building qualify. Secondly, does the lease qualify. Thirdly, does the tenant qualify. In order for the building to qualify, it must be a 'house'. This has developed a wide definition and can mean a shop with a flat above, or a building converted to flats. However, one essential feature is that there must be no material over or under-hang with an adjoining building (if there is, then it is likely to be a flat).

The lease must comprise the whole of the house and it must be a long tenancy, i.e., a lease with an original term of more than 21 years. However, if it is a business tenancy, then it will not qualify if it is for an original term of 35 years or less.

The tenant must have owned the lease of the house for a period of at least two years before the date of the claim. Prior to the 2002 Act, it was also necessary for the tenant to occupy the house as his only or main residence for a three year period. The residence test has now been abolished save in limited circumstances.

If a house is mixed use so that there is a business tenancy (for example a building comprising a shop with a flat above) or if the house includes a flat which is subject to a qualifying lease under the 1993 Act (see above), then the tenant is still required to fulfil a residence test. However, it is modified so that the tenant has to occupy the house as his only or main residence only for two years or periods amounting in aggregate to two years in the preceding ten years.

Prior to the 2002 Act, the personal representatives of a deceased tenant had no right to make a claim., even where the deceased tenant was able to fulfill the qualifying conditions. However, such personal representatives can now make a claim provided that the right is exercised within a period of two years from the date of grant of probate.

The Price

The 1967 Act has three different valuation methods. In every case, the valuation date is the date of the claim.

If the house qualified pre-1933 (i.e. by not needing to rely on amendments made to the financial limits and/or low rent conditions by either the 1933 Act, the 1996 Act or the 2002 Act) and had a ratable value of less than £1,000 (£500 outside the Greater London Area) on 31st March 1990 then the valuation is under section 9(1). This section expressly excludes any marriage value and restricts the value to a proportion of the site value.

If the house qualifies pre-1933 but did not have a ratable value of less than £1,000 (£500 outside the Greater London Area) on 31st March 1990, the valuation is under section 9 (1A). The valuation elements here are:

- The capitalised value of the landlords ground rent and the value of his reversion (being the present freehold vacant possession value deferred for the unexpired lease term; and
- 50% of the marriage value (the additional value released by the tenants ability to merge the freehold and leasehold interests) must be to the landlord although the marriage value will be deemed to be nil if the lease has an unexpired term of more than 80 years at the date of the claim.

If the house qualifies post-1933 (i.e. the claimant needs to rely on amendments made to the financial limits/low rent conditions by either the 1933 Act or the 2002 Act) then the valuation is under section 9 (1C). This is broadly the same as section 9(1A) valuation except that the freeholder can be compensated for loss in value of other property owned by him, including development value, consequent on the severance of the house from the other property.

How do I claim?

The procedure for a claim is relatively straightforward. The tenant serves his notice of claim, which is in prescribed form and needs to state (inter alia):

- • a description of the house – but not necessarily with a plan;
- • particulars to establish that the lease and tenant qualify;
- • what the tenant thinks is the basis of valuation.

In addition to the price and the tenant's own legal costs and valuation fees, he will be required to reimburse the freeholder his legal costs and valuations fees. The landlord is likely to respond with a procedural notice requiring payment of a deposit (equal to three times the rent payable under the lease) and asking the tenant to deduce title and (if a residence test is relevant) to produce evidence by statutory declaration that he fulfils the residence condition.

The landlord's valuer is also likely to inspect the house for the purpose of carrying out a valuation. The Act requires the landlord to state, within two months of the notice of claim being served, whether or not he admits the claim. If the claim is not admitted then the tenant must decide if he wishes to dispute the rejection through the courts. A freeholder cannot resist a claim on redevelopment grounds.

Disputes.

If the claim is admitted and either the terms of the conveyance or the price remain in dispute after two months following the date of the notice of claim, then either party can apply to the leasehold valuation tribunal for the matter in dispute to be determined. There are no time limits on the making of this application.

Completion

Once the terms of the conveyance and the purchase price have been agreed or determined by the leasehold valuation tribunal, the matter reverts to a conveyancing transaction with the parties proceeding to completion.

The tenant can withdraw at any time up to one month following the determination of the purchase price. Unlike collective enfranchisement and statutory lease extension claims, there are no strict procedural time limits. However, the tenant is liable for the landlord's costs as from the date of his notice of claim.

The extended lease option

The 1967 Act also allows the qualifying tenant of a house to take an extended lease of the house for a term of 50 years to expire after the term date of the existing lease at a modern ground rent throughout the extended term and without payment of a premium. This right has been little exercised in recent years not least because none of the amendments relating to the abolition of financial limits and the low rent test introduced by the 1993 Act, the 1996 Act and the 2002 Act apply to it. Furthermore, the extended lease originally had no statutory protection and carried no right to acquire the freehold.

However, following the 2002 Act, all tenancies extended under the 1967 Act now have security of tenure. Furthermore, the tenant under an extended lease now has the right to acquire the freehold, if he otherwise fulfils the qualifying conditions; in such cases, the purchase price will be determined in accordance with section 9(1C) but with modified assumptions.

****

HOUSING LAW GENERALLY

16

RELATIONSHIP BREAKDOWN AND HOUSING RIGHTS

When a relationship breaks down, whether the people in question are married or not, problems can often occur in relation to the property that was home. The rights of people will depend mainly on whether they are married or not, whether there are children involved and the legal status of individuals in the home.

Housing rights in an emergency

In the main, it is women who suffer from domestic violence. This section refers to women but the rights are the same for men.

If you are women and have been threatened by a man and are forced to leave your home then there are several possibilities for action in an emergency. The first of these is either going to a women's refuge. These provide shelter, advice and emotional support for women and children. These refuges will always try to admit you and as a result are sometimes crowded. They will always try to find you somewhere to live in the longer term. Refuges have a 24-hour telephone service if you need to find somewhere. For addresses see *useful addresses* at the back of this book.

Approaching the council

A person suffering domestic violence who has been forced to flee can approach the local council and ask for help as a homeless person. Councils will demand proof of violence and you will need to get evidence from a professional person, such as doctor or social worker or police. The council decides whether or not it has a duty to help you and you should seek advice if they refuse. Some councils, but not all will offer help to battered women.

If you are accepted as homeless then the council should not send you back to the area where the violence began.

Obtaining a court order

Another course of action in an emergency is to obtain a court order against the man you live with. Courts can issue orders stating that a man:

- Should not assault you or harass you
- Not to assault any children living with you
- To leave the home and not to return
- To keep a certain distance from your home or any other place where your children go regularly.
- To let you back in your home if you have been excluded.

If you believe a court order would help you should get advice on where to find a solicitor or law centre that deals with these types of applications to the court. Certain orders are harder to get than others, such as exclusion orders. Matters need to be very serious indeed before such an order will be made. However, you will be advised of this when approaching a solicitor or law centre.

Failure to obey the terms and conditions laid down in the order can lead to arrest for contempt and a fine or even imprisonment.

Long term rights to the home

Long term rights to stay in a home depend on a number of circumstances. If you are married and the ownership or tenancy of the property is in joint names you have equal rights to live in the property. If it is owned then you will have a right to a share of the proceeds if it is sold. In certain circumstances have a right to more (or less) than a half share, or to the tenancy in your name after divorce.

If you are married but the ownership or tenancy is in one name only there are laws to protect the rights of the other party. Courts have the power to decide who has the ownership or rights over the matrimonial home, even if the property is held in one persons name only. This can also apply to people who were married but are now divorced and to those who were planning to get married within three years of their engagement.

Spouses who are not the owner or tenant of the home have a right to stay there. The court has the power to exclude either of the spouses, even if they are sole or joint owner or tenant. If your husband has left and stopped paying the rent or mortgage payments, the landlord or building society is obliged to accept payments from you, if you wish to make them, even if the property is not in your name. If the home is owned by your husband then you can register your right to live in it. This prevents your husband selling the home before the court has decided who should live there. And also prevents him taking out a second mortgage on the property without your knowledge. This is known as 'registering a charge' on the home. The court also has the power to transfer a fully protected private tenancy, an assured tenancy or a council or housing association tenancy from one partner to another.

If the matrimonial home is owner occupied and proceedings have started for a divorce, the court will decide how the value of the property will be divided up. The law recognises that, even if the property is in the husbands name only, the wife has a right to a share in its value, that she often makes a large unpaid contribution through housework or looking after children and that this should be recognised in divorce proceedings. The court looks at a number of things when reaching a decision:

- The income and resources of both partners
- The needs of you and your husband
- The standard of living that you and your husband had before the marital breakdown
- Ages of partners and length of marriage
- Contributions to the welfare of the family
- Conduct of partners

- Loss of benefits that you might have had if the marriage had not have broken down.

The court also has to consider whether there is any way that they can make a 'clean break' between you and you husband so that there are no further financial ties between you.

In certain circumstances, the court can order sale of the matrimonial home and the distribution of proceed between partners.

If you are not married

If you are not married then your rights will depend on who is the tenant or the owner of the home.

Tenants

If a tenancy is in joint names then you both have equal rights to the home. You can exclude your partner temporarily as we have seen by a court order. If you are a council tenant then you may want to see if you can get the council to rehouse you. You should get advice on this from an independent agency (see useful addresses).

If the tenancy is in your partners name only then the other person can apply for the right to stay there, for their partner to be excluded or for the tenancy to be transferred.

Home owners

If you live in an owner occupied property you and you partner may have certain rights to a share of the property even if you are not married.

If the home is jointly owned then you have a clear right to a share in its value. If one person has contributed moiré than the other then a court can decide that an equal share is unfair. The court cannot order the transfer of the ownership of property but it can order the sale and distribution of the proceeds.

If the home is in one persons name there is no automatic right to live in the home, even if there are children. However, a solicitor acting on your behalf can argue that by virtue of marriage and contribution you should be allowed to stay there and be entitled to a share.

****

17

THE LAW AND MOBILE (PARK) HOMES

Introduction to park homes

Park Home is the commonly used term for a mobile home (caravan) on a protected site within the meaning of the Mobile Homes Act 1983 (the 1983 Act). A protected site is one that is required to be licensed by a local authority under Part 1 of the Caravan Sites and Control of Development Act 1960 which covers most sites containing wholly residential park homes or a mixture of residential and holiday homes.

If someone has an agreement to live in a 'park home' as their only or main residence on a protected site then they will have the benefit of the rights and protections provided by the 1983 Act which implies a number of important terms into their agreement. These cover such matters as to how the agreement can be terminated, how the annual 'pitch fee' can be changed and the process that needs to be followed when buying or selling (or gifting) the home.

Changes to implied rights under the 1983 Act came into effect on 26 May 2013. These concern the buying, selling or gifting of a park home and the pitch fee review process. Further changes to the licensing of park homes came into effect on 1 April 2014, giving local authorities greater powers to enforce compliance with site licence conditions.

LEASE (see useful addresses) can advise on issues concerning park homes whether you are a park home owner, site owner or a local authority.

The right to a written agreement and a statement of rights

The site owner must give you a statement of your legal rights and the terms of your agreement. The agreement cannot change your rights under the Mobile Homes Act. You or the site owner can apply to change the terms of the agreement within six months of the issue of the original agreement. Either side can apply to the county court or an arbitrator, if they cannot agree the terms. You should always check the agreement for the terms of payment and fees and if not happy apply to change them.

Buying a park home from the site owner

The recent changes made by the Mobile Homes Act 2013 will have little impact upon the process of purchasing a park home from the site owner. Where you are buying a park home directly from the site owner (or bringing your own home onto the site) you can seek to negotiate the terms of your agreement with the site owner, although certain terms will be implied into the agreement by the 1983 Act.

What you should receive

The site owner should provide you with a written statement setting out the specific terms of your agreement to live in your park home on the site. This must be given to you 28 days before you sign the agreement (or if there is no such agreement at least 28 days before occupation).

The terms of the written statement will apply whether or not they are part of any written agreement with the site owner.

The form of the written statement has been prescribed by regulations. The latest version is contained in the Mobile Homes (Written Statement) (England) Regulations 2011 which applies to written statements provided after 30 April 2011.

The written statement contains information about your rights and the particulars of your agreement such as the details of the pitch on which the park home rests, the pitch fee, The terms that are implied into the agreement under the 1983 Act including repairing responsibilities and any additional express terms that it is proposed should be included in the agreement. If you don't receive a written statement then any express terms in the agreement such as those providing for the payment of the pitch fee cannot be enforced by the site owner. You can apply to a tribunal for an order that the written statement is provided by the site owner. The form that should be used is Form PH1.

Other rules

There will often be specific rules that will apply to your particular site (site rules) which deal with such matters as any age restrictions, the use of car parking areas and keeping pets.

Changing the terms of the agreement

You or the site owner can apply to a tribunal to delete, vary or add an express term within the first six months of the original agreement being made. The form that should be used is Form PH2.

Buying a park home from an existing home owner

Significant changes have been made by the Mobile Homes Act 2013 to the process by which a mobile home is bought and sold in England following changes made by the Mobile Homes Act 2013. These changes mean that as from 26 May 2013 a buyer does not have to have any contact with the site owner before buying the home.

You should note that until changes are made to the law that applies in Wales, the consent of the site owner will still be required for you to purchase a park home there.

What will be the terms of your agreement with the site owner?

You will be taking over an existing agreement with the site owner and so this will depend upon the particular agreement that was previously made with the site owner for the home to be stationed on the site. However certain terms will be implied into your agreement and these are the terms that were referred to at the beginning of this guide.

The new process for buying a park home in England

New terms concerning the sale of the park home are now being implied into agreements between park home owners and site owners. These new implied terms vary depending on whether the home was acquired by the current owner on or before 26 May 2013.

However the changes that have been introduced will mean that in all cases the site owner will have no direct involvement in the sale or gift of a park home and any inconsistent provision in the agreement or site rules will not be enforceable.

The process

Once you have agreed with the seller to purchase the park home, the seller will be required to serve you with a prescribed notice called a Buyer's Information Form at least 28 days before the sale date. This notice will include prescribed information including the proposed sale price and details about the pitch fee and the site owner.

The other documentation that the seller must also give you is set out in the above Buyer's Information Form and includes the agreement, site rules, evidence of charges payable for utilities and any survey of the park home.

If the current home owner acquired their park home before 26 May 2013, you and the seller will be required to send to the site owner a Notice of Proposed Sale Form containing your name and, if the site has rules, confirmation that you will comply with any site rules concerning age restrictions, the keeping of pets and the parking of vehicles.

The sale can go ahead if the seller does not receive a notification within 21 days of the service of the Notice of Proposed Sale Form that the site owner has applied to a tribunal for a Refusal Order on the grounds that you will not comply with these rules, or there is insufficient evidence of compliance. The seller will have to transfer the pitch agreement (this is called the Assignment) to you. Both of you will need to complete an Assignment Form which provides confirmation of the agreed purchase price, the commission payable to the site owner and the pitch fee payable by the new occupier.

You will be required to provide the site owner with details of the seller's forwarding address when you notify the site owner that you are the new owner of the home. You must therefore ensure that the seller provides you with a forwarding address.

You will need to retain 10% of the purchase price to pay to the site owner, although this does not become payable until the site owner has provided his bank details following the service of the Notice of Assignment (see below).

Please note that there will be no need to inform the site owner of the sale where the home was acquired by the seller after 26 May 2013. Within seven days of the assignment, you must complete and send a Notice of Assignment form to the site owner with documentary evidence of the price paid for the park home.

As soon as is practicable after receipt of the Notice of Assignment, the site owner must provide you with details of their bank account into which the commission should be paid. The payment of the commission does not become due until the site owner has provided you with his bank details. On receipt of the details, you will have seven days to pay the commission into the site owner's bank account.

Commission on the sale

It is an implied term under the Mobile Homes Act 1983 that the site owner is entitled to receive a commission on the sale of a park home at a rate not exceeding 10% of the sale price.

You (the buyer) must retain 10% of the purchase price to pay to the site owner although this does not become payable until the site owner has provided his bank details.

Gifting a park home to family member

The Mobile Homes Act 1983 enables a park home owner to assign their agreement with the site owner to a member of their family (this is defined in the Mobile Homes Act 1983 and includes spouse, parent, child, grandparent, grandchild and brother or sister). The changes introduced by the Mobile Homes Act 2013 to the process whereby a park home in

England can be gifted to a family member mirror those for the sale of a park home. This means that the site owner is not required to approve the gift and any inconsistent provision in the agreement or site rules will not be enforceable.

Please note that until changes are made to the law in Wales, the consent of the site owner will be required for a gift of a park home to a family member there.

The new process for receiving a gift of a park home in England

What documentation should be provided to the family member to whom it is proposed to gift the park home? You should receive a copy of the agreement, site rules, evidence of the charges payable for utilities and any survey of the park home as for a normal sale (although there is no requirement for the current occupier to provide you with the Buyer's Information Form).

Informing the site owner about the gift of the home

Where the current occupier (the family member gifting the home to you) acquired the park home before 26 May 2013, they will need to complete and send a Notice of Proposed Gift to the site owner providing details of how you are related to him or her, together with supporting documentary evidence such as a birth or marriage certificate.

Where there are site rules concerning the age of the occupant, the keeping of pets and the parking of vehicles, the person making the gift will need to provide information to the site owner confirming that you are able to comply with these rules.

The family member gifting the park home can then proceed with the assignment provided that he has not been informed by the site owner within 21 days of the service of the Notice of Proposed Gift that an application has been made to a First-tier Tribunal (Property Chamber) for a Refusal Order, or if he has already been informed that there is no objection to the proposed gift.

You should note that this stage will not be necessary where the home is acquired after 26 May 2013.

The family member gifting the home will have to transfer the pitch agreement (this is called the Assignment) to you. Both of you will need to complete and sign an Assignment Form. You must also ensure that your family member gifting the home to you provides you with a forwarding address.

Is there anything else that needs to be done?

The final stage is for you to complete a Notice of Assignment which you as the new owner must send to the site owner within seven days of the assignment.

No commission will be payable on the gift of a park home to a family member

Protection from eviction

The Mobile Homes Act 1983, as amended by the Housing Act 2004, gives owners the right to keep their homes on the site they occupy indefinitely. There can only be a fixed time limit on the agreement if the site owner's planning permission, or right to use the land, is itself limited to a fixed period. If the time limit is later extended, then so is your right to stay there. The resident can bring the agreement to an end by giving at least four weeks notice in writing. The site owner can only bring the agreement to an end by applying to the county court or to an arbitrator. There are only three grounds on which the site owner can seek to end an agreement:

- You are not living in the mobile home as your main residence.
- The mobile home is having a detrimental effect on the site because of its age or condition or is likely to have this effect within the next five years. The site owner can only try to use this ground for ending the agreement once in any five-year period, starting from the date the agreement began.

- You have broken one of the terms of the agreement and the court or the arbitrator thinks it is reasonable to end the agreement. The site owner must first tell you that you have broken the agreement and give you a reasonable time to put things right.

If the site owner can prove to the court or the arbitrator that the agreement should be brought to an end for one of these reasons, the site owner can then get an eviction order from the courts. Arbitrators cannot make eviction orders. The site owner can normally go to court to end the agreement and for an eviction order at the same time.

If the site is privately owned, the court can suspend an eviction order for up to one year, but cannot suspend it if the site is owned by the local council. It is a criminal offence for the site owner to evict you without a court order, to harass or threaten you or to cut off services such as gas, electricity or water in order to get you to leave.

The site owner can only make you move to another part of the site if:

- Your agreement says that this can be done
- The new pitch is broadly comparable to the old one
- The site owner pays all the costs.

Other rights and obligations-Charges-Pitch fee

You have to pay a 'pitch fee' to the park owner to rent the land your park home sits on. The park owner can propose to change it once a year. They must give you 28 days' notice in writing. You or the park owner can apply to a tribunal to decide the pitch fee if you can't agree on it.

Gas, water, electricity and liquefied petroleum gas (LPG)

The Office of the Gas and Electricity Markets (Ofgem) sets the amount the park owner can charge you for gas and electricity. The park owner can't charge you more for gas and electricity than they paid for it, including any connection charges. For water, the park owner can only charge what the water company charges and a reasonable administration fee. Charges for LPG aren't regulated.

Park improvements

If the park owner plans to make improvements, they must:

- give you at least 28 days' notice in writing and let you know how you can comment on the plans
- tell you if it will affect your pitch fee

They can go ahead with improvements even if most residents disagree. The park owner can sometimes recover improvement costs through a pitch fee increase. If you disagree, you can apply to a tribunal. Contact the Leasehold Advisory Service for advice.

Residents' associations

You can set up a 'qualifying' residents' association to represent home owners in the mobile home park where you live. Qualifying residents' associations have certain rights and park owners should consult the residents' association when they want to spend money on improvements or change how they run the park.

Park owners must give at least 28 days' notice of any changes and take the association's concerns into account before they make changes.

Setting up a qualifying residents' association Your association must include at least half of the home owners in your park. Residents who rent their homes can't join. You'll have to keep certain records and documents, like:

- an up-to-date list of members
- a constitution
- any other rules of the association

You'll have to elect a:

- chairman
- secretary
- treasurer

The chairman, secretary and treasurer can make administrative decisions. Members should vote on all other decisions. You need to ask the park owner to 'acknowledge' your association. You can apply to a tribunal if they refuse. They can order the park owner to acknowledge your association. Your association can continue to meet if it doesn't meet the qualifying conditions but the park owner won't have to talk to the association about park operations and management.

7. Settling disputes

If you have a dispute with the park owner that you can't work out, you can apply to a tribunal. Decisions made by the tribunal are legally binding. If your agreement says you must use an arbitrator, ignore it. You must use a tribunal instead. The tribunal can settle certain disputes, eg:

- changing a residence agreement
- changing the pitch fee
- moving a park home
- damage and repairs to the site
- transferring ownership of a park home to someone else

Getting Help

Contact the Leasehold Advisory Service for advice if you're not sure whether you have a case. Call the tribunal if you have any questions about completing the form. The tribunal can't give you legal advice.

Tribunal Service

Telephone: 0845 600 3178
Monday to Thursday, 9am to 5pm
Friday, 9am to 4.30pm

Renting a park home

You have a rent contract if you pay rent to a landlord. It doesn't have to be in writing. If you don't have a written contract you should be able to stay for a year from the date you moved in even if you don't have anything in writing.

If you have a written contract

A written contract should say how long you can live in your home. During this time your landlord can still ask you to leave if:

- your contract says they can ask you to leave with 4 weeks' notice
- you break the rules ('terms') of your contract and it says the owner can ask you to leave as a result

When your contract ends

Your landlord can ask you to leave as long as they give you 4 weeks' notice. If you don't leave the owner can ask the court for an 'eviction order' which forces you to leave.

If your landlord tries to evict you

If your landlord tries to evict you (force you to leave), you'll have more rights to stay if you live on a 'protected site'.

A protected site is a mobile home park which has planning permission to have residents living there throughout the year. A holiday park isn't a protected site. Your right to stay also depends on:

- what your rental contract says
- whether your home is counted as a 'dwelling house', which means you have rights from tenancy laws
- To be a dwelling house your park home must be:
- your permanent residence – where you live most or all of the time
- connected to mains electricity or water

- unmovable or so large that it can't be moved in one piece, eg you can't drive it or tow it away yourself

Types of tenancy

The type of tenancy you have depends on the date you moved in and started paying rent. You will have:

- a regulated tenancy if you moved in and started paying rent before 15 January 1989
- an assured or assured shorthold tenancy if you moved in and started paying rent on or after 15 January 1989

Getting advice

Tenancy rights can be complicated and depend on your situation. You should get legal advice if you think your landlord is treating you unfairly.

You can also contact Citizens Advice, the Leasehold Advisory Service or charities such as Shelter or Age UK if you have questions. See useful addresses.

****

18

RESIDENTIAL HOUSEBOATS-GENERAL ADVICE

Houseboats

Living on a houseboat may be a more affordable option than buying or renting a flat or house. This section looks at some of the issues to consider, such as how to pay for a houseboat and where to moor it. You may be able to get help from a marine finance specialist to buy a houseboat. Before you buy a houseboat, check you can moor it somewhere. You may be able to claim housing benefit to help with costs

Buying a houseboat

If you are buying a houseboat, there are a few things you should consider.

Finance

You cannot get a mortgage to buy a houseboat from a high street bank or building society. If you can't buy outright, you may have to approach a marine finance specialist who charge higher rates of interest and are unlikely to lend you more than 80 per cent of the purchase price. The repayment term is likely to be 15 years.

You may not to be able to borrow to fund the purchase of a sea-faring houseboat unless the loan can be secured on a home that you already own.

Buyer beware

Houseboats do not come with title deeds in the same way that houses do. If you are planning to buy a houseboat, make sure that the seller actually owns the boat and has a legal right to sell it. If you don't check, you could lose all your money and your houseboat.

Survey

You should get a survey done by someone who is an expert in houseboats, unless you know a lot about the subject. You don't want to buy a houseboat only to discover later that you are sinking.

Houseboats don't always come with running water, electricity, gas, central heating, telephone points, an address or rubbish collection. You should consider how to access services that are essential to you. Heating is particularly important, as life on the water can be very cold.

Residential moorings for houseboats

If you plan to live on your houseboat, you need to find a residential mooring. You can rent a residential mooring from the local council or a private landlord. You'll probably need to sign a rental agreement with your landlord, giving you both certain rights and responsibilities. Make sure you read the agreement carefully first.

Cruising moorings are only intended for people who are cruising the waterways. They are not intended for people to moor houseboats on a permanent basis.

If you cannot find a residential mooring for your houseboat, you can apply to the council as homeless.

Renting a houseboat

If you rent a houseboat, make sure that it is being rented to you with a residential mooring. Most residential moorings do not allow houseboats to be rented out, so make sure that your landlord has permission for you to stay there. The usual rules regarding security of tenure apply. A Citizens Advice Bureau will advise you further.

Paying council tax for a houseboat

You have to pay council tax if you live on a houseboat with a residential mooring.

Claiming housing benefit when living on a houseboat

If you live on a houseboat, you can claim housing benefit to help pay your mooring fees and rent, if you rent rather than own it.

****

19

AGRICULTURAL TENANCIES

If you rent agricultural land or buildings to run a farm business you may have an agricultural tenancy agreement. Every agricultural tenancy agreement is unique. We refer here to 2 types of agricultural tenancies governed by legislation:

- Farm Business Tenancies governed by the Agricultural Tenancies Act 1995 - those agreed after 1 September 1995
- 1986 Act Tenancies governed by the Agricultural Holdings Act 1986 - those agreed before 1 September 1995

Farm Business Tenancies

A tenancy is a Farm Business Tenancy if at least part of the tenanted land is farmed throughout the life of the tenancy. The tenancy must also meet one of these 2 conditions:

- if the tenancy is primarily agricultural to start with, the landlord and tenant can exchange notices before the tenancy begins confirming they intend it to remain a Farm Business Tenancy throughout - this lets tenants diversify away from agriculture where the terms of the tenancy agreement allow this
- if the landlord and tenant don't exchange notices before the tenancy begins, the tenancy business must be primarily agricultural to be considered a Farm Business Tenancy

Farm Business Tenancy rent reviews

Landlords and tenants can negotiate their own rent levels and decide whether or not they want to have rent reviews. Either the landlord or tenant can demand a rent review every 3 years by law.

However, landlords and tenants can agree on how often a rent review should take place – this agreement replaces the law. For example, you can agree on a rent review every 4 years.

You must not preclude a reduction in rent in your rent review agreements.

Farm Business Tenancy compensation

As a farm business tenant you're entitled to compensation at the end of a tenancy for:

- physical improvements you've made to a holding (provided the landlord has given consent to the improvements)
- changes that increase the value of the holding (provided they are left behind when the tenant leaves)

You can agree in writing an upper limit on the amount of compensation, usually equal to the tenant's cost in making the improvements.

Ending a Farm Business Tenancy

Landlords and tenants of a Farm Business Tenancy can end the tenancy by issuing a notice to quit. The minimum notice period to quit is 12 months

1986 Act agricultural tenancies

Agricultural tenancies agreed before 1 September 1995 are known as 1986 Act Tenancies. They're also sometimes referred to as Full Agricultural Tenancies (FATs) or Agricultural Holdings Act tenancies (AHAs).

These tenancies usually have lifetime security of tenure and those granted before 12 July 1984 also carry statutory succession rights, on death or retirement. This means a close relative of a deceased tenant can apply for succession to the tenancy within 3 months of the tenant's death.

Applying for succession stops any notice to quit given by the landlord on the tenant's death. Two tenancies by succession can be granted, so it's possible for the tenant's family to work the holding for 3 generations.

Farmers with a tenancy granted before 12 July 1984 can also name an eligible successor such as a close relative who can apply to take over the holding when they retire.

1986 Act Tenancies rent reviews

The landlord or tenant has the right to a rent review 3 years after either the:

- start of a tenancy
- previous rent review

If land is added to or removed from a holding then the next rent review must be either at least 3 years from one of the following:

- the date the original tenancy began
- from the date of the previous rent review for the original tenancy

This rent review must happen even if the rent has changed to reflect changes to the amount of land on the holding.

1986 Act Tenancies compensation

Under the 1986 Act Tenancy agreements the tenant is entitled to compensation at the end of their tenancy for the following:

- major long-term improvements
- short-term improvements
- 'tenant right'

Major long-term improvements
These include:

- making or planting water meadows
- planting orchards
- erecting or altering buildings
- constructing silos, roads or bridges
- repairs to fixed equipment

Short-term improvements
These include:

- mole drainage
- protecting fruit trees against animals
- clay burning
- liming and chalking of land
- applying manure, fertiliser, soil improvers and digestate to the land (in England)

'Tenant right'
These include:

- the value of growing crops
- the costs of husbandry, such as sowing seeds and cultivations
- compensation for disturbance where a landlord terminates the tenancy with a notice to quit

The amount of compensation is measured by the increase in value to the holding made by the improvements. The landlord may also claim compensation for disrepair - usually the cost of repairing any damage.

Dispute procedures

Where a landlord or a tenant has a dispute relating to an Agricultural Tenancy (either a 1986 Act Tenancy or a Farm Business Tenancy) they can use third-party expert determination or arbitration procedures.

Arbitration is the private legal settlement of a dispute by an independent, professional arbitrator which can involve either of the following:

- a tribunal hearing where both sides present evidence and testimony
- the 2 parties agreeing to resolve the dispute using written arbitration procedures, avoiding the time and costs of a hearing

If a landlord and tenant can't agree on the appointment of an arbitrator, either of them can apply to the President of the Royal Institution of Chartered Surveyors (RICS) to make an appointment on their behalf for an arbitrator to:

- decide a rent review dispute
- resolve a dispute other than a rent review

You must pay RICS for this service – the forms explain the fees.

Contacts

Farmers can get further information on agricultural tenancy issues from the Tenant Farmers Association and the National Farmers Union.

Landowners can get further information from the Country Land and Business Association.

****

Index